The
Collected
Poems of
Montagu Slater

The
Collected
Poems of
Montagu Slater
edited by
Ben Harker

STACK
BOOKS

Smokestack Books
1 Lake Terrace,
Grewelthorpe,
Ripon
HG4 3BU

info@smokestack-books.co.uk

www.smokestack-books.co.uk

ISBN 9781739173012

Smokestack Books
is represented
by Inpress Ltd

# Contents

Introduction                                           9

**Part I Poems**
An Elegy                                              33
Love, We Can Lie Back                                35
Cock Crow                                            36
The Ebb and Flow of the Moon                         37
The Fear                                             38
Incitement to Disaffection: a Fragment               39
In the Beginning: *A Broken Narrative*               40
The Hunter and the Hunted                            46
Where My Bones Rest                                  47
The Ambassador                                       48
A Ballad from Korea                                  49
Character Equals Situation                           50
Exercise with a Broad Nib                            51
Helen Was Not Up Was She                             52
Now Praise...                                        53
The Obituary                                         54
The Answer                                           55
The Pitfall                                          56
St Venus's Eve                                       57
A Sentence of Judges                                 58
The Spirit Kills                                     59
To Chloe with an Old Valentine                       60
When I Awake                                         61
Untitled                                             62
Iboland                                              63
A Dark Place under the Trees                         64
This is our Love Child                               65
Men and Women Almost Equal                           67
On a 17th Century Painting                           68
Royal Academy: Special Exhibition                    69
Your Touch Has Still                                 71
Past Years                                           72

**Part II Songs and Choruses from Dramatic Works**

Ballad from 'Domesday' (1933)                                75
Speech for a Fascist from 'Cock Robin' (1934)                77
Chorus from *Easter* 1916 (1936)                             79
Mother Comfort: a Song for Two Female Voices (1936)          80
Chorus from *Stay Down Miner* (1937)                         81
Deleted Song from *Stay Down Miner* (1937)                   83
Chorus from a Pageant (late 1930s?)                          84
Chorus from 'Towards Tomorrow' (1938)                        85
Chorus from 'An Agreement of the People' (1942)              87
A Verse for Arthur Benjamin (1946)                           88

**Part III Libretti and Poetic Dramas**

The Seven Ages of Man (1938)                                 91
Old Spain (1938)                                            101
*Peter Grimes* (1945)                                       105
Deleted 'Mad Song' from *Peter Grimes* (1945)              152

Notes                                                       153

# Introduction

Montagu Slater (1902–56), the quietly prolific communist man of letters, has disappeared almost without trace. Other communists of his generation wrote voluminous autobiographies. Slater, a 'small, delicate man' who 'almost hid even while talking', was never drawn to self-revelation.[1] There is no book-length biography, and Slater left behind little of the material – letters, diaries, even photographs – upon which one might be based (he burned a tranche of papers in or around 1950).[2] Even the British state, who vigilantly surveilled many in his circle, seem to have overlooked the inconspicuous Slater (no MI5 file has yet come to light). Bigger names and characters became synonymous with the interwar documentary film movement in which he was a leading figure.[3] Discussion of his most significant work, the opera he created in collaboration with Benjamin Britten, *Peter Grimes* (1945), makes minimal mention of him.[4] His plays are largely forgotten, his novels long out of print, and little of his poetry has been published to date.[5] Who, then, was Montagu Slater?

### Early Years

Charles Montagu Slater (1902–1956) was born into a family of Wesleyan Methodists on 23 September 1902 in Millom, a Cumbrian port-town shaped and scarred by the mining and working of iron.[6] His mother, Rosa Annie Thora Lugsdon, ran the family – there were five children – and his father, Seth Slater, a lay preacher, was a master clothier and sub-postmaster (Seth's tailor's shop doubled as the town's only post office). Charles, always known by his middle name, was educated at Millom secondary school. The socio-political setting of his youth was 'collapsing trade, strikes, returning soldiers' and 'begging in the streets.'[7] A clever child, he won a rare scholarship to Oxford and went up to read Philosophy, Politics and Economics, as a non-collegiate student, in 1920, the year that the Communist Party of Great Britain was formed. His Oxford contemporaries and associates included young intel-

lectuals radicalized by the October revolution – Tom Wint-
ringham, Ralph Fox – who would loom large in the CPGB in the
years ahead.

After graduation, Slater took a job as reporter for the
*Liverpool Post*. He lived in a dockside dormitory, and became
active in the city's labour movement, joining the Communist
Party, probably in 1927. These experiences informed a long,
never completed cycle of poems provisionally entitled 'The
Venereal Hypothesis', whose heroic couplets struggled to inte-
grate classical erudition and the seamier details of dock-side
life.[8] In 1928 he married photographer Enid Mace, with whom
he would have three daughters, and the couple moved to
London. Slater worked on Fleet Street for the *Morning Post* –
the preferred broadsheet of Britain's officer-class – but chan-
nelled energies into grassroots activism for the National Union
of Journalists and his Communist Party branch. Rising long
before work to write, he completed two novels, both published
by the small, prestigious Wishart Press in the early 1930s. *The
Second City* (1931) looked back to Liverpool and went largely
unreviewed. The critically-acclaimed, Berlin-set *Haunting
Europe* (1934) looked forward, grappling with the spread of
international fascism and the challenge of creating a 'new and
emancipated society' from within 'the very body of a tyrannical
and reactionary State.'[9]

### Left Review

Slater and his culturally-minded comrades were convinced that
Britain was not impervious to fascism, and that its culture, a
weathervane of prevailing winds, showed signs of it.[10] A new
politically-oriented cultural journal was needed to rally counter
energies. *Left Review* was launched in October 1934 as the offi-
cial organ of the British Section of the Writers' International. The
journal was jointly edited by Slater, Tom Wintringham and
Amabel Williams-Ellis, but Slater, above all, set the tone over the
fifteen months in which he was an editor. He staked out core
positions in a series of articles, some written under the
pseudonym 'Ajax', to which he would hold for the rest of his
life.[11]

He rejected the idea that cultural work could be bracketed off from politics. Culture, rather, defined, challenged and enlarged the consciousness and perception upon which politics depended.[12] Likewise, 'theoretical advance' was a condition rather than an impediment of 'literary advance'; serious writers needed theory to see through surface phenomena to underlying structures.[13] He had patience neither with the fetishization of all things Soviet, nor with fantasy – fashionable in the early 1930s – that an authentic 'proletarian' culture could be invented 'from scratch' without assistance from the 'bourgeois' cultural past or intellectual strata.[14] The serious task was the recovery, territorialization and development of progressive elements in the national culture, 'making the stored up literary labour of the past usable by the present.'[15] The process of defining and transmitting national culture, he insisted, was always political (it decided what, and who, counted, and did not); the custodians of culture naturally defined it in their own image. In particular, the gate-keeping elite had undervalued and sidelined a powerful current of demotic folk poetry: John Skelton, *Piers Ploughman*, William Blake, music hall, penny dreadfuls, popular theatre, folksong, psalmbooks, proverbs and jokes. Countering the myth that 'folk poetry' ended with the Renaissance would be a central concern of Slater and his networks.[16] He had already begun this work by seeking out, editing and republishing the scripts of Victorian barnstormers, *The Demon Barber of Fleet Street: A Traditional Acting Version* (1928), *Maria Marten or Murder in the Red Barn* (1928) and *Two Classic Melodramas* (1933), activities that would continue across the next two decades.[17]

### Documentary

For Slater in the mid-1930s, documentary was a key form, especially if trained on working-class life and struggle. Capitalist society, ran the logic, was a tissue of lies. Its survival depended upon the concealment of its enabling violence and robbery, home and abroad. To 'describe things as they are' was therefore 'a revolutionary act', especially economic exploitation lived beneath the radar of the dominant culture.[18] Outlined in *Left Review*, this theory was practised in *Coal Face* (1935), a short documentary film for which Slater wrote the narration, produced by General Post Office Film Unit and directed by the Brazilian-born leading light of the 1920's French avant-garde, Alberto Cavalcanti. Slater's first collaboration with the young composer Benjamin Britten, *Coal Face* synthesized arresting visuals – shots of miners hewing underground, conveyors, headstocks, despoiled countryside, desolate pit villages – and a richly varied soundtrack of Britten's modernist music, industrial sound effects, chanting voices and choral song (poet WH Auden supplied a short lyric). Though funded by the coal industry, the film effectively foregrounded the exploitation and alienation of the workers and communities integral to Britain' 'basic industry' and helped to crystallize a new, radically-charged 1930's documentary aesthetic.[19]

Slater now experimented with documentary modes across multiple forms. He reworked his day-job coverage of the occupation by miners facing redundancy of the Nine Mile Point Colliery in Monmouthshire, 1935, as a book of eye-witness reportage, published as *Stay Down Miner* (1936). A forgotten classic in the tradition of JB Priestley's *English Journey* (1934) and George Orwell's *The Road to Wigan Pier* (1937), the book detailed not only the strike but a tight-knit way of life defined by 'the bearing of dignity and stiff chapel-going independence' reminiscent for Slater of Millom.[20] Drama, however, was Slater's primary form in the mid to late 1930s. Two plays sounding a caution against Anglicized forms of fascism – 'Domesday' (1933) and 'Cock Robin' (1934) – were written but not formally staged.[21] His experiments soon found a receptive network in Left Theatre (1934–37), a professionally-based organization convinced that 'the very class which plays the chief part in contemporary history' was 'debarred from expression in the present-day theatre.'[22] Keen to balance its programme of predominantly international plays with British material, Left Theatre coordinated a playwriting competition in 1935, won by Slater with *Easter 1916*, a drama reconstructing the 'actualities' of the rising which gave expression to Slater's longstanding interest in the politics of Ireland.[23] With a score by Britten, and support from the North London Area Committee of the

Amalgamated Engineering Union, the play was staged at Islington Town Hall and the Phoenix Theatre in December 1935, and published by the Communist Party's press, Lawrence & Wishart, the following year.[24]

Next Slater reworked *Stay Down Miner* as a documentary play, again with a score by Britten, performed at the Westminster Theatre in May 1936, followed by a short tour of London community halls in early November under the title New Way Wins.[25] Reviews were mixed.[26] But this was a prolific spell for Slater, enthused by, and in demand from, the expanding cultural networks of the Popular Front left, which now included the Artists' International Association, the Workers' Music Association, the Left Book Club, and Unity Theatre, the latter now settled into its permanent premises in King's Cross. At Unity, Slater worked on two signature 'living newspapers' of the late 1930s, *Busmen* (1937) and Crisis (1938).[27]

## Pageantry, Puppetry

A central priority of these networks at a moment of political crisis was to challenge culturally dominant accounts of national history – of the type commonly broadcast by the BBC – that foregrounded King and country, airbrushed out radical political movements, and, it was argued, primed the ground for the consolidation of the political right.[28] Struggles over the country's past, present and possible future were duly fought out in many contexts in the late 1930s, including the form of the popular pageant. This was a portmanteau genre typically combining song, poetry, documentary and dramatic vignettes that appealed to Slater, and he scripted four pageants between 1937 and 1939. A lampoon of typical Empire Day pageantry, Slater's 'Pageant of Empire', written for a Left Theatre Revue, was performed with music by Britten at Collins Music Hall in February 1937.[29] 'The Pageant of South Wales' was commissioned by the South Wales Miners' Federation and the Labour Research Department. Performed simultaneously on May Day 1939 in Pontypool, Abertillary and Ystradgynlais, the production involved 6000 actor participants and represented the region's working-class struggle from the Newport rising to the present.[30]

'Heirs to the Charter', staged at the ice-hockey arena of the Empress Hall, Earl's Court, in July 1939, drew an audience of 9000, and presented the Communist Party as the culmination of a tradition of working-class struggle stretching back to Chartism.[31] The largest production, 'Towards Tomorrow', was commissioned by the London, Watford and South Suburban Co-operative Societies to mark the sixteenth International Co-operative Day, and was staged at Wembley Stadium in early July 1938.[32] A collaboration between Slater, composer Alan Bush, and producer André van Gyseghem, the pageant drew upon 3,000 performers, attracted an audience of 78,000, and replotted national history as a cycle of oppression and resistance. Fore-grounding the growth of the Co-operative Movement between 1844 and the First World War, Slater's script culminated in a finale insisting that the movement's core values – democracy, freedom, peace, social solidarity – remained fundamental to the struggle for a 'new tomorrow' ('Life can be what you make it') in late 1930s Britain.[33]

The mass spectacle of the Popular Front pageant, where the usual boundaries between actors and audiences were sugges-tively dissolved in anticipation of a radically reordered culture, provided Slater with a large canvass to express core convictions around national history, actual and potential. The miniaturism of the puppet-show, by contrast, created space for close-up study of communities and situations, and Slater produced libretto-type scripts for two short plays staged at the Mercury Theatre, Notting Hill in July 1938 by Binyon Puppets, the trav-elling company run by artist, writer and puppeteer Helen Binyon. Drawing on Millom memories, 'The Seven Ages of Man' dramatized life's stages in a northern mill community. Through a combination of homespun philosophizing, dialogue, dance and risqué song, the piece insisted that, far from univer-sal, these stages were shaped by the structures of class and gender. 'Old Spain' used four puppets to dramatize the dream-life of a young man haunted by the Spanish Civil War, and by the possibility of volunteering for active service ('We are caged in death. / Bring knives to free us' appealed one of the women embodying Spain's suffering).[34] In the absence of productions scripts or detailed newspaper reviews, the performances are not easy to visualize, but they marked a deepening relationship with Britten, who wrote and performed piano music for the puppet show, rehearsing in Slater's north London flat, remembered by friends as a bustling, happy home filled with children, pets, photography equipment, and books.[35]

## Peter Grimes

Slater was unfit for military service on medical grounds. During the early war period he divided his time between three jobs: journalism (theatre critic and sub-editor at the Co-op's Sunday weekly, Reynold's News); Head of Scripts at the Film Unit of the Ministry of Information; and the Army Bureau of Current Affairs, where he worked first on films, then on living newspapers performed to the troops.[36] His working relationship with Britten was now firmly established, and in 1942 they collaborated on a new pageant, 'An Agreement of the People', performed by the Co-operative Society at Wembley.[37] Second only to novelist Christopher Isherwood – who was too busy – Slater was Britten's preferred librettist for a new project, an opera to be based on *The Borough* (1824) by poet and Aldeburgh curate, George Crabbe, (1754–1832). Crabbe's poem, first drawn to Britten's attention by an EM Forster essay in *The Listener*, atmospherically captured what Britten called the 'grim and exciting seacoast' of the composer's native Suffolk, especially in the story of the reclusive fisherman Peter Grimes, an enigmatic figure ostracized by the community for the alleged mistreatment of his young apprentices.[38] Having visited Britten in Suffolk to 'get atmosphere' in May 1942, Slater began writing, with the composer, as Slater put it, acting as a director shaping the process.[39] Slater re-worked the 'Peter Grimes' section of Crabbe's poem as a three-act verse drama, set 'towards 1830', to be performed by a cast of fourteen, plus chorus. He replaced Crabbe's five-beat line – 'out of key with contemporary modes of thought and speech' – with a more idiomatic four-beat line, and Crabbe's ringing couplets with a 'rough rhyme' – 'assonance and consonantal rhyme' – by way of striking the balance between structure and naturalness.[40] Britten was pleased with Slater's approach, and progress.[41] The libretto was completed by the end of September 1942. Britten, busy with other projects, began to compose the music in January 1944.[42]

The well-documented problems that blighted the collaboration began a year later when Britten, nearing the end of the composition, began to visualize the opera more fully. One issue was dramatic emphasis, also a question of genre. Crabbe's verse realism powerfully communicated Grimes' agitated psychological state.[43] Britten identified strongly with the socially alienated central figure, around whom rumour clung, and would later draw parallels between Grimes the outsider and his own life as a homosexual and conscientious objector in a world hostile to both groups.[44] He was keen that the opera should tease out the questions around Grimes' background, psychological make up and sexuality implicit in Crabbe's text.[45] Slater, wary of the potentially melodramatic effect of too narrowly focusing on Grimes, preferred to retain Crabbe's unsettling ambiguity around the central character, stressing instead Grimes' place in the community by developing the other characters, especially Ellen Orford, the schoolmistress and widow Grimes hoped to marry.[46] Britten liked this emphasis,[47] but was increasingly drawn to a type of operatic symbolism dramatizing an alienated figure hounded by a conformist society.[48] Slater was sceptical, and a new phase of what Britten diplomatically called 'discussions, revisions and corrections' ensued, sharpened when Britten showed the libretto to Eric Crozier, who would direct the first production of *Peter Grimes* at Sadler's Wells in June 1945.[49] Crozier remembered the librettist as 'a silent, rather recalcitrant figure' during some tense meetings.'[50] At this point Britten, who had already considered that Auden might help to revise the libretto, asked poet Ronald Duncan to write alternative verses for the contentious final scene, which were used.[51] Slater agreed to changes that did not compromise his authorship of the text. The production went ahead, playing to full houses, and critical acclaim.[52] To the consternation of Britten, Slater then published his original libretto – 'the one to which the music was composed' – in his first and only verse collection, *Peter Grimes and other Poems* (1946).[53] It was a controversial move that drew attention to the divisions and, in asserting the identity of the libretto as a freestanding work, disregarded the usual hierarchy of librettist and composer.[54] Slater would receive criticism from Britten scholars in the years to come.[55] In the meantime, he and Britten worked together on an already commissioned film, *Instruments of the Orchestra* (1946), made by the Crown Film Unit for the Ministry of Education, before parting company.[56] The libretto for Britten's next opera, *The Rape of Lucretia* (1946), was written by Duncan.

## Cultural Upsurge

The framework for much of Slater's work in the late and immediate post-war years was the conviction that the so-called 'cultural upsurge' of wartime Britain, in which access to the arts had begun to be broadened – in part through state-funded initiatives (CEMA, ENSA, ABCA) – must be sustained and developed in the image of a better, socialist, future.[57] Communists were at the forefront in 'upsurge' initiatives, notably through the magazine *Our Time*, whose readership would peak at 18,000.[58] Slater became theatre editor in 1946, and enthusiastically detected a 'new wind blowing' through British theatre with mass demobilization.[59] He supported these fresh energies in *Our Time, Theatre Today* – a short-lived, glossy conspectus of the theatre world which sold up to 20,000 copies – and through his own writing for the stage.[60] Here he developed key concerns – recovering and affirming radical history, reconnecting labour and culture – in the new context. He was active in the trade-union funded company 'Theatre 46', and the season of new plays it staged at Fitzrovia's Scala Theatre, for which he wrote *A Century for George*, a three-act prose play directed by Bernard Miles telling the story of the Amalgamated Engineering Union (AEU) on its silver jubilee.[61] The 1948 centenary of *The Communist Manifesto* was another significant anniversary; Slater scripted a musical pageant performed at the Albert Hall on 30 March 1948 in collaboration with the British Communist Party's leading composers (Rutland Boughton, Alan Bush, Christian Darnton, Bernard Stevens), and a shorter piece staged by Merseyside Unity Theatre as 'The Centenary of the Communist Manifesto', at the Liverpool Philharmonic in June 1948.[62]

He also returned to writing fiction in the 1940s, sometimes with an eye on paying the bills. While working on *Peter Grimes*, he had written the commercially-oriented, *Once a Jolly Swagman* (1944), a novel that keyed into the popularity of speedway racing, a sport Slater enjoyed.[63] The novel became a feature film in 1948, starring Dirk Bogarde, scripted by William Rose and directed by Jack Lee.[64] He wrote *Who Rides a Tiger* (1947), an espionage novel tracking an MI5 agent as the hot war gave way to the cold, and *The Inhabitants* (1948), partly set in a version of Millom, that contrasted the empty lives of a languid, upper-class London elite and the bustling vitality of a northern working-class community in which 'friendliness was the single key'.[65] His most ambitious work of the late 1940s was *Englishmen with Swords: A Narrative of the Years 1647–1648 and 1649* (1949). A radical historical documentary, this novel took the form of a journal supposedly written by journalist Gilbert Mabbot, official licensor of the press between 1647 and 1649 and secretary of Sir Thomas Fairfax. Animated by the ideas thrown up during these revolutionary years – rulers' rights to rule, the ethics and implications of property ownership, the possibility of social levelling, the radical extension of the franchise – the novel atmospherically recreates the period of the Putney Debates, the second Civil War and Charles I's execution.[66]

## Cold War

Reticent by nature, Slater was no outspoken critic of insular trends that stiffened within British communism as the Cold War deepened. He was at least, however, conspicuously absent from the most reductive initiatives, and wrote nothing that he would later have cause to regret. Indeed, as cultural communism's range contracted, Slater's widened. At a time of widespread anti-Americanism on the left, he prepared a 500-page anthology to mark the centenary of the death of one of his favourite writers, Edgar Allan Poe.[67] Mediating diplomatically, he challenged the tone, if not the logic, of a party increasingly bent on ideological conformity during the so-called 'Caudwell Controversy', in which the 'idealist' deviations of Christopher Caudwell's posthumously published theoretical work were ritualistically denounced.[68] And as many of the key cultural institutions and initiatives of the Popular Front and People's War periods either fractured or contracted – the Left Book Club, the Artists' International Association, the Workers' Music Association – Slater kept channels open. He renewed the collaboration with his old GPO Film Unit associate, director John Grierson, writing the critically-acclaimed documentary-style feature film, *The Brave Don't Cry* (1952), which dramatized the struggle of miners trapped by a landslide at the Knockshinnoch Castle Colliery in September 1950.[69] He was highly active in the Authors' World Peace Appeal, an organization established in 1951 to challenge a deteriorating Cold War 'climate of opinion infected by fatalism, apathy and fear' and, in particular, culture that presented a third world war as inevitable.[70] He was equally prominent in the writers' union, PEN, co-editing with non-communists Roy Fuller and Clifford Dyment *New Poems 1952: A PEN Anthology* (1952), the first of a series of books to showcase new work in a form seldom commercially viable, and now struggling with the closure of key periodicals (*Horizon, New Writing*).[71] He wrote features for the broad-brow *Picture Post* on subjects ranging from Sir David Lindsay, to novelist Emma Smith, to the passing of the National Parks Acts.[72] New work expressed a longstanding interest in psychology and the causes and treatment of mental illness: he scripted *Out Of True* (1951), a short documentary drama film stressing the treatability of mental breakdown, sponsored by the National Health Service (a version of his script was published as *Cure of Minds* (1952)); and he co-wrote multiple versions of a never-staged play about Sigmund Freud.[73] While other communists in his circle visited the so-called 'People's Democracies', and produced romanticized accounts, Slater drew inspiration from visits to Africa in the early 1950s, and became increasingly interested in the history and politics of the continent.[74] He wrote a never-published novel, 'The Women's War', set in an imaginary British protectorate, and a long poetic travelogue about Iboland, Nigeria, the beginning of which he published.[10] While completing his final book, *The Trial of Jomo Kenyatta* in 1955, which sifted 2000 pages of court transcripts to lay bare the sharp practice of colonial justice at work, he was planning a new prose work on Ghana.[76]

## Final Years

Slater's productivity seemed to increase as his health deteriorated; the stomach cancer he suffered before the war returned, and he developed heart trouble in the early 1950s. He resumed work with composers. For Bernard Stevens he wrote the libretto for a full-length opera, 'Mimosa' (the music was never completed), and the song cycle 'The Palatine Coast', published in 1952.[77] In the last year of his life, he wrote a libretto for an opera, 'Yerma', based on Lorca's play of the same name, for composer Dennis ApIvor (completed but never performed).[78] He wrote and pitched projects for film (a feature about Swansea's Italian steelworkers) and television (a play about Ned Kelly), and worked on a new poetry collection.[79] He was admitted to hospital in the weeks following the Soviet invasion of Hungary, 'not at all a bad time in history to get away and think', he put it, with characteristic dryness.[80] Like his work ethic, his communism remained intact, redefined in 1954 as the 'full community of all minds and possessions' necessary for 'complete freedom.'[81] One can only speculate about the forms and allegiances that his politics would have taken in the post-1956 period, but his closest associates – Edgell Rickword, Randall Swingler, Bernard Stevens, Arnold Rattenbury – were drawn to the New Left, a movement that credibly claimed Slater's long career – nondogmatic, open to a wide range of cultural influences and forms, committed to cultural democracy – as a valuable antecedent.[82] The fifty-four year old Slater died in Whittington Hospital, Islington, London, on 19 December 1956.

## The Poems

*The Collected Poems of Montagu Slater* is the first book of Slater's poetry published since *Peter Grimes and other Poems* (1946), and includes work written across the 1930s, 1940s and 1950s. The book also reflects Slater's poetic range, both in terms of theme (place, love, illness, art, people, politics, travel) and form (predominantly traditional, with more experimental flourishes, especially in the 1930s). The book's three sections reflect the different contexts for which he wrote poetry: first, the mainly shorter poems conceived as freestanding texts to be read off the page; second, songs for musical setting and poems and songs embedded in dramatic productions; third, the verse dramas and libretti, two for puppets ('The Seven Ages of Man', 'Old Spain') and one for the opera house ('Peter Grimes'), all previously published in *Peter Grimes and other Poems* (1946). Within these sections, the material is sequenced more or less chronologically, although, as many of the previously unpublished poems are undated, the ordering is not in all cases an exact guide to composition date.

The first section draws upon multiple sources. Two selections of Slater's poems were curated and published posthumously by his friends and associates, the first by Edgell Rickword and John St. John for *The New Reasoner* in 1958, the other by Arnold Rattenbury, who knew Slater better than most – he had lodged with the family in the 1940s – for *Renaissance and Modern Studies* in 1976. Most of the poems included in those selections are re-published here, although the texts have been checked against the originals in the Montagu Slater Papers at the University of Nottingham Special Collections, and modified where necessary. A handful of poems are reprinted from newspapers and periodicals including *Left Review* and the *New Statesman*, and the 'Ibo sequence' is reproduced from the *1952 PEN Anthology*. The remainder of the poems are from the Slater Papers, and have never been published before. Poems have been left out if there is no clear evidence that Slater considered them finished. For reasons of space, a small number of other poems – especially the very early 'Venereal Hypothesis' work and the remainder of the 'Ibo Sequence' – have also been excluded. The second and third sections reproduce all the material from *Peter Grimes and other Poems,* minus 'The Figure of Nobody', a work written partly in prose, with additional material added from various playscripts. I am very grateful to staff at the University of Nottingham Special Collections, the Working Class Movement Library, Salford, and the John Rylands Library, Manchester, for all their assistance with this project. Thanks to Bridget Kitley for permission to publish her father's work. Special thanks to Andy Croft of Smokestack Books for commissioning this book, and for his good-humoured help in bringing it to completion.

Ben Harker,
University of Manchester

## Notes to Introducton

1   Arnold Rattenbury, Introduction to Slater, *Englishmen with Swords* (1949: London: Merlin, 1991), p. vi, p. xii.

2   Rattenbury, 'Poems by Montagu Slater', *Renaissance and Modern Studies* XX (1976), p. 121.

3   Marsha Bryant, *Auden and Documentary in the 1930s* (Charlottesville: University of Virginia Press, 1997).

4   Michael Kennedy, Britten (London: Dent, 1981); Donald Mitchell, with the assistance of John Evans, *Benjamin Britten, 1913–1976* (London: Faber, 1978).

5   A rare exception is Steve Nicholson, 'Montagu Slater and the Theater of the Thirties' in Patrick J Quinn ed., *Recharting the Thirties* (Selingsgrove, PA: Susquehanna University Press, 1996), pp. 201–20. Only one novel, *Englishmen with Swords*, has ever been reprinted; he published one novel, the thriller, *Man with a Background of Flames* (1954), under the pseudonym Richard Johns.

6   Biographical information drawn from Rattenbury, 'The Poems' and Introduction to *Englishmen*; JB (Jack Beeching?), 'Montagu Slater', obituary in *World News*, 19/1/57, pp. 41-2; Robert Brown, entry in *Oxford Dictionary of National Biography*, <u>Slater, (Charles) Montagu (1902–1956), writer and librettist</u>; John St. John, 'Montagu Slater, A Group of Poems', *New Reasoner* (Spring 1958), pp. 80–81.

7   Rattenbury, 'Introduction', p. viii.

8   Archived in Tw T 1/1/1-18, Literary Papers and Correspondence of Charles Montagu Slater, Special Collections, University of Nottingham. Hereafter, Slater Papers.

9   Slater, *Haunting Europe* (London: Wishart, 1934), p. 285; Edwin Muir, 'New Novels', The Listener, 2/5/34, p. 768; RD Charques,

'Haunting Europe', TLS 24/4/34, p. 296.

[10] Edgell Rickword, 'Straws for the Wary: Antecedents to Fascism', Left Review (October 1934), pp. 19–23; Douglas Garman, 'What?...The Devil', pp. 34–37; Charles Madge, 'Pens Dipped in Poison', pp. 12–17.

[11] Ajax, 'The Writers' War', *Left Review* (November 1934), pp. 13–17; Slater, 'Controversy, Writers' International', *Left Review* (January 1935), pp. 125–28; 'The Purpose of a Left Review', *Left Review* (June 1935), pp. 359–66; 'The Turning Point', Left Review (October 1935), pp. 15–21.

[12] Ajax, 'Writers' War', p. 16.

[13] Slater, 'Purpose', pp. 362–24.

[14] Middle class intellectuals were dismissed by some as 'the vast jellyfish of the petty middleclass'; 'the jellyfish has a place in our kettle', Slater insisted. Slater, 'Controversy', p. 127.

[15] Slater, 'Controversy', p. 127.

[16] Slater, 'Turning Point', pp. 18–19.

[17] Followed up with *Barnstormer Plays* (London: John Lane, 1943), *Round the World in Eighty Days: A Stage Spectacle Adapted from the Novel by Jules Verne* (London: John Lane, 1951) and Thomas William Robertson the Elder's Victorian comedy drama, Caste (London: John Lane, 1951).

[18] Slater, 'Purpose', p. 365.

[19] Storm Jameson's essay, 'Documents', for instance, saw documentary films like *Coal Face* as a model for a socialist literature. Fact 4 (1937), pp. 9–18.

[20] Slater, *Stay Down Miner* (London: Martin Lawrence, 1936), p. 79.

[21] 'Domesday', Slater Papers, Tw T 1/2/9; 'Cock Robin' (Tw T 1/2/28) was possibly performed as part of a Left Theatre Revue.

[22] Undated Left Theatre Handbill, Lawrence & Wishart Records, 1927-51, GEN MSS 703, Box 3, Beinecke Library, Yale University; Colin Chambers, The Story of Unity Theatre (London: Lawrence & Wishart, 1989), pp. 33–34.

[23] Slater, *Easter 1916* (London: Lawrence & Wishart, 1936), p. 13.

[24] Slater, *Easter 1916*, p. 7; reviewed by Douglas Garman, 'Montagu Slater's Easter', *Left Review* (January 1936), p. 180.

[25] Published as *New Way Wins: The First Published Version of the Play Originally Entitled Stay Down Miner* (London: Lawrence & Wishart, 1937).

[26] *The Times* and the *Telegraph* were critical; *Left Review* found the play hard to follow, and considered that cast of eight struggled to convey the importance of the wider community to the occupation. LA Butt, 'Stay Down Miner', *Left Review* (June 1936), p. 476; newspaper reviews in Times (12/5/36) and Telegraph (11/5/36) cited in Donald Mitchell ed., *Letters from a Life: The Selected Letters and Diaries of Benjamin Britten 1913-1976. Volume II, 1923-1939* (London: Faber, 1991), p. 416, p. 430.

[27] Chambers, Unity Theatre, pp. 140-60, 163-65.

[28] Typical was the BBC's lavish 1936 St George's Day broadcast, 'An English Pageant', billed as 'a succession of soldiers and statesmen, cathedrals and villages.' Editorial, *Radio Times* 17/4/36, p. 3; George Audit, 'May Day, The English Spirit, Some Utopias', Daily Worker, 27/4/36.

[29] Britten thought it 'hilariously funny.' Mitchell ed., Letters II, p. 478; Britten's diary 25/4/37, quoted in Donald Mitchell, Philip Reed and Mervyn Cooke eds., *Letters from a Life: The Selected Letters and Diaries of Benjamin Britten 1913-1976. Volume III, 1946-1951* (London: Faber, 1991), p. 68.

[30] Mick Wallis, 'Heirs to the Pageant: Mass Spectacle and the Popular Front' in Andy Croft ed., *A Weapon in the Struggle: The Cultural History of the Communist Party of Great Britain* (London: Pluto, 1998), p. 57. This paragraph also draws on Mick Wallis, 'Pageantry and the Popular Front: Ideological Production in the 'Thirties', *New Theatre Quarterly* 38 (May 1994), pp. 132-56.

[31] Wallis, 'Heirs', pp. 61-62.

[32] Chambers, Unity, p. 138.

[33] Wallis, 'Heirs', pp. 54-57.

[34] Slater, *Peter Grimes and other Poems* (London: Bodley Head, 1946), p. 72.

[35] Harold Hobson reviewed it in the *Observer*, 26/6/38, 'Puppet Show 1938', quoted Mitchell ed., Letters II, p. 478; Brown, DNB; Rattenbury, 'Introduction', p. xii.

[36] Slater, 'Ann as I remember her', *Nothing is Lost: Ann Lindsay*,

1914–1954 (London: Communist Writers' Group, nd (1954)), p. 5.

[37] Slater had also written 'Mother Comfort', the first of Britten's *Two Ballads for Voices and Piano*, performed at the Wigmore Hall in December 1936, and published the following year (the other text was Auden's 'Underneath an Abject Willow'; Britten dedicated his Spanish Civil War cantata, 'Ballad of Heroes' (1939), to the Slaters Humphrey Carpenter, *Benjamin Britten: A Biography* (London: Faber, 1992), p. 123; Carpenter, Britten, p. 174, 177; Chambers, Unity, p. 246.

[38] Britten, Introduction to Eric Crozier ed., *Benjamin Britten: Peter Grimes* (London: Sadler's Wells / John Lane, 1946), p. 7; Forster's essay, 'George Crabbe: The Poet and the Man', originally published in *The Listener* (29/5/41), is reprinted in the volume, pp. 91–94; Mitchell et al, *Letters III*, p. 92.

[39] Slater, Preface, Peter Grimes, p. 7; Mitchell ed., Letters II, p.1050.

[40] Slater, 'Preface', p. 7; Slater, 'The Story of the Opera', Crozier ed., p. 19.

[41] Slater, Britten said, had 'taken to Grimes like a duck to water.' Mitchell ed., *Letters II*, p.1037.

[42] Mitchell ed., *Letters II*, p.1089, p. 1181.

[43] Grimes 'toiled and railed' and 'groaned and swore alone.' Howard Mills ed., George Crabbe, *Tales, 1812 and Other Selected Poems* (Cambridge: CUP, 1967), p. 110.

[44] Britten in interview with Michael Schafer (1963), reprinted in Paul Kildea, ed., *Britten on Music* (Oxford: OUP, 2003), p. 226.

[45] Britten's partner, Peter Pears, who would play Peter Grimes in the first production, talks of Grimes' 'queerness.' Mitchell ed., *Letters II*, p.1189.

[46] The claim made by later commentators that Slater, as dogmatic Marxist, flattened Grimes into an expression of class forces—'the poor working-class fisherman (...) driven to violence by the iniquitous class system' as one of Britten's biographers puts it—is not borne out by the libretto, which owes more to Freud—about whom Slater later wrote a play—than to Marx (as in Crabbe's poem, Grimes' father looms large in Slater's libretto). Carpenter, *Britten*, p. 181. Slater's beleaguered Grimes believes that material success would secure social 'esteem' and the 'freedom from pain' at 'gossip's tale', but this is by no means a Marxist insight. Slater, *Peter Grimes*, p. 35.

[47] Carpenter, *Britten*, p. 181; Britten endorse the idea of 'an opera about the community, whose life is "illuminated" for this moment by the tragedy', but was concerned that without exploration of Grimes' inner life, the fisherman might appear 'just a pathological case—no reason and not many symptoms.' Mitchell ed., *Letters II*, p. 1037, 1131.

[48] An argument made by Philip Brett, '"Grimes is at his Exercise": Sex, Politics, and Violence in the Librettos of Peter Grimes' (2000), reprinted in Philip Brett, *Music and Sexuality in Britten: Selected Essays* (Berkeley: University of California Press, 2006), pp. 34–53. Another key work on these revisions is by Philp Brett, 'Peter Grimes: The Growth of the Libretto' in Paul Banks ed., The Making of Peter Grimes: Essays and Studies (Woodbridge: Boydell, 1996), pp. 73–78.

[49] Britten quoted in Banks ed., *The Making*, p. 2; Carpenter, Britten, p. 214. The sticking point was Grimes's 'mad scene' soliloquy in Act III Scene II. Slater's text was short and linked Grimes' mental state to memories of his dead father. Britten wanted a longer passage that underscored Grimes' social alienation and reprised key themes to set up the musical crescendo. Mitchell ed., *Letters II*, p. 1243; Carpenter, Britten, p. 217.

[50] Donald Mitchell, 'Montagu Slater (1902–1956): who was he?', Philip Brett ed., *Benjamin Britten, Peter Grimes* (Cambridge: CUP, 1983), p. 37.

[51] Carpenter, Britten, p. 180, p. 217; both versions are reproduced in Mitchell ed., *Letters II*, p. 1280.

[52] *Picture Post* saw the production as marking 'the reinstatement of opera in the musical life of this country'; there was consensus that Peter Grimes would 'outlive' the young Britten, still in his early thirties. Carpenter, *Britten*, p. 224, p. 223.

[53] Slater, Peter Grimes, p. 7. The other poems were the puppet plays, choruses from *Easter 1916* and *Stay Down Miner*, and 'The Figure of Nobody', which drew upon the late 1920s poems. The key letter is Britten to Slater, 28/8/45. Mitchell ed., *Letters II*, p. 1279.

[54] Brett, 'Sex, Politics', p. 40.

[55] 'All the evidence' sums up Donald Mitchell in his editorial comments to Britten's letters, 'suggests that' Slater was 'a preternaturally slow, cautious worker who did not find it easy to respond speedily or perhaps to understand the needs and priorities of a composer.' Mitchell ed., *Letters II*, p. 1280. The first point sits

uneasily with the letters exchanged: Britten was clearly delighted with the speed of Slater's work—working three jobs Slater produced the libretto in five months—while sometimes frustrated by his own progress. The trajectory of Slater's career, distinctive for its work with musicians, calls the second assertion into question. Leading Britten scholar Philip Brett gives Slater credit for preventing the opera from being what Britten himself termed 'nothing more than a rather bloodthirsty melodrama.' Brett, 'Sex, Politics', p. 40.

[56] Mitchell ed., *Letters II*, p. 1289–90.

[57] Analysed in Ben Harker, *The Chronology of Revolution: Communism, Culture and Civil Society in Twentieth-century Britain* (Toronto: University of Toronto Press, 2021), pp. 38–76.

[58] Harker, *Chronology*, p. 87; Launched back in February 1941 and briefly edited by Slater during the war, Our Time gradually broadened its cultural scope through a commission of specialist sub-editors. Our Time extended the work of both *Left Review* (1934–38) and the short-lived periodical of the Left Book Club's Poetry Group, *Poetry and the People* (1938–1940), and carried forward a particular emphasis on supporting working-class creation and enjoyment of poetry. Slater wrote an article for the first issue celebrating the poetry of songs written by servicemen. Slater, 'Bless 'em All: A Piece about Army Songs', *Our Time* (February 1941), p. 25.

[59] Slater, 'Theatre in 1946', *Our Time* (January 1947), p. 135.

[60] Contributors included Eric Bentley, Basil Dean and Sylvia Townsend Warne Andy Croft, 'The Boys Round the Corner: The Story of Fore Publications' in Croft ed., *Weapon*, pp. 151–52; copies in Slater Papers, Tw T 1/5/1.

[61] Yvonne Kapp, 'Art and the AEU', *Our Time* (April 1948), pp. 178–80.

[62] Walter Holmes, 'The Manifesto has its 100th Birthday', *Daily Worker* 31/3/48; Andy Croft, *The Years of Anger: The Life of Randall Swingler* (Abingdon: Oxford, 2020), p. 233n7; Souvenir programme; Centenary of the Communist Manifesto, Liverpool Philharmonic, 27/6/48, Slater Papers, Tw T 2/2/2.

[63] Unsigned, 'Speedway Rider', TLS, 16/12/44, p. 609.

[64] Slater wrote his own screenplay, which was not used. Slater, 'Once a Jolly Swagman', (9/3/47), Slater Papers, Tw T 1/4/1.

[65] Jack Beeching wrote 'one marvels at the cleverness but is quite unmoved.' Beeching, 'Recent Novels', Our Time (May 1947), p. 227;

Slater, *The Inhabitants* (London: Bodley Head, 1948), p. 126.

[66] John Edward Bowle, 'Cromwell's England', TLS 19/11/49, p. 746.

[67] Slater ed., *The Centenary Poe: Tales, Poems, Criticism* (London: Bodley Head, 1949).

[68] Analysed in Harker, *Chronology*, p. 277 n130.

[69] Screenplay dated October 1951, *Slater Papers*, Tw T 1/4/9.

[70] Handbill, 'Introducing the Author's World Appeal', Labour History Archive and Study Centre, People's History Museum, Manchester, CP ORG/MISC/ 03/09.

[71] Clifford Dyment, Roy Fuller, Hermon Ould, Montagu Slater, Letters to the Editor, TLS 25/5/51, p. 325; the same letter appeared in the Listener, 24/5/51, p. 840; the collection was reviewed by Alan Ross, 'Poetic Impulses of Our Time', *TLS* 29/8/52.

[72] Slater, 'The Three Estates', *Picture Post*, 10/9/49, pp. 31–32; 'Emma Smith settles in', *Picture Post*, 29/4/50, pp. 39–42; 'They queued to climb up Snowden', *Picture Post* 22/4/50, pp. 40–44.

[73] Slater Papers, Tw T 1/2/11–15.

[74] 'A lad plays the accordion to a table-full of railway-workers, and sings folk-ballads while the sun filters through the acacia-leaves.' Jack Lindsay and Maurice Cornforth, *Rumanian Summer: A View of the Rumanian People's Republic* (London: Lawrence & Wishart, 1953), p. 43.

[75] 'The Women's Wars', Slater Papers, Tw T 1/3/13; Slater Papers, 'Ibo Sequence', Tw T 1/1/49/1–36; Dyment, Slater and Fuller eds., *New Poems* 1952, pp. 90–93.

[76] 'Memorandum: The Birthpangs of Ghana' (1955), Tw T 1/3/6; Slater, *The Trial of Jomo Kenyatta* (London: Secker & Warburg, 1955).

[77] Slater Papers, Tw T 1/1/108.

[78] Draft in Slater Papers, Tw T 1/2/3/1–201; related correspondence, Tw T 1/2/4/1–6.

[79] Slater Papers, Tw T 1/3/1-21; Arnold Rattenbury, 'Montagu Slater: A Rough Bibliography' (22/2/76); a shortened version of this was published in *Renaissance and Modern Studies* by Rattenbury, who oversaw the archiving of Slater's papers. Thanks to Andy Croft for sharing with me the full, unpublished, version.

[80] JB (Jack Beeching?), 'Montagu Slater', obituary in *World News*, 19/1/57, pp. 41–2.

[81] Slater, 'Ann as I remember her', p. 7.

[82] EP Thompson saw Slater and his circle as antecedents of the New Left: *'Left Review'* (1971) and 'Edgell Rickword' (1979) in Thompson, *Persons & Polemics* (London: Merlin, 1994), pp. 228–44.

# Part I
# Poems

# An Elegy

*Written in the shadow of a mountain in a northern mining port*
*which, established in the Nineteenth Century, proves*
*superfluous to the needs of the Twentieth.*

When the last candle of the day gives over
its conflagration of the quivering air
and riven with curtains of the west discover
endless tranquillity projected there:

and the sun drowns in continents of wests,
earth, redolent of shadow, never free
from sun's corrosion, till his lusty breasts
touch the horizon of a menstrual sea –

Mountain, whose rondure is determinate
by riches of your still unshafted mines,
chambers and galleries and caves intestate,
a various hoard which every twig divines:

the glimmering presence of your urgent Jove
your shoulder hummocking above the screes
where smoky clouds bend daylight as it moves
to closure in imperfect cadences

tells how an earthquake had once split the rock
and giant sparks leaping the centuries
found the dead shafts and mines of human thought
and legends of imaginary countries.

Our little lives, our chapels and our hymns,
mining and fishing – apostolic round –
a tidal river governed with its whims
neap tides renew but spring tides leap the bounds.

Once, annually, our men forsook their trade,
Hired wagonettes to where the rocks begin
climbed through the night to ambuscade
the earliest secret of the rising sun;

to see the inhuman world open its eyes,
screes at their feet and laminated shale,
on the north-west the Cumbrian mountains rise
and to the south the glimmering peaks of Wales.

And then returning to their normal lives
found that their minds were overshadowed by
a memory of the mountain, and their wives
discovered in them puzzling sympathy.

Now solemn the precedent shadow falls,
like disintoxication, like dismay
of clocks set going after drinking brawls
with unrelenting news of yesterday

and down the dream-choked gullet of the street
crab-like on an ambiguous journey led
we read in all the faces that we meet
stale news, a preterite of the nearer dead.

And being mindful of the twilight mood
and the grave charm of the alternate note
the lyric burden of this solitude,
satyricon for any golden throat;

we hold the drowsy magic of the form
till the full cycle of the song disposes
that voices rhythm-cheated of the norm
in the old dark repeat the older closes.

And touch, which is the lovers' sense, implies
a membrane's pleasure when a last bird sings
of night's scarce-scented guesses, and the eyes
give up their kingdom over all visible things.

# Love, We Can Lie Back

Love, we can lie back and laugh or cry now,
Having killed our demon like Tobit with his fish.
Love, we have finished with hopes and guesses.
The past is accomplished and we ignore the future.
And you may live on, but I – I may as well depart now.
Love, it is begotten or it is not begotten.
Your flower-like flesh accepts the ambiguity,
Your nakedness native to earth as any plant,
And the trees welcome your essence to their company.
So you may live on but I – I may as well depart now.
And if it is a male child, pricked with this self-same lack
That shuts him from the idleness of trees and animals
(For even a dog in rut has no place in the sun
But grey activity bare and unmetaphored)
Live on Lillith and do not be too sorry when he also departs.

# Cock Crow

The cock crows twice. I turn and toss
Dreaming the honeysuckle is so sweet
I can imagine it in sleep.
But when the cock crows I am lost.

I dread the meaning of his trumpet
From the high-gardened sleep and grieve
That coming of the day should heave
Away the contemplative blanket.

Here is another day to dress
The ruffled feathers, the brown egg
In clucking wonder to be laid.
Energy is unhappiness

Unhappiness but homing here,
Here in the garden, here the bee
Homes to the honeysuckle tree.
But the cock crows a thought too near.

The world turns... am I afraid?
I can feel conscience multiplied
By chiding voices millionfold
Cock-crowing now, 'Have you betrayed?'

The cock crew twice, crew twice. I know
One more summons is permitted
By tradition of the city.
Cock crow cock crow cock crow cock crow.

# The Ebb and Flow of the Moon

The ebb and flow of the moon is now
A shuttle that imprisons you
Setting your being to a tune
Governed by the ebb and flow of the moon.

The crescent moon, a pallid ghost
Stares bleakly on a naked coast
Sets in the twilit afternoon
Rises laboriously at dawn.

Third quarter is the false attempt;
For truth is great but it was meant
To prevail only when the mind
Swims like a cork on the spring tide.

Fourth quarter, hush, the night is long
The hushed sea whispers to the moon
That leans on a reflective breast.
Sing lullaby the flooded coast.

## The Fear

Labourers and tradesmen are
The population of this star
And the solar system turns
On labouring and trading terms.

Gravitation's mystic bonds
May be measured in foot-pounds
And fixed stars raise from ancient graves
Old light like capital reserves.

Attraction – ah! the lover's debt –
Centrifugal curves offset,
And the old dissatisfaction
Is moon-hidden by rotation.

Nebulae and Milky Way –
In between them wise men say,
In blank spaces of the sky
Lurks the fear of bankruptcy.

# Incitement to Disaffection: A Fragment

Forming up in the street
As if apologising for being there, soldiers
Very bright-eyed, Ben going up to a double file remembering the
next door banjo when Deacon's soldier son strummed all day
long only 17 then at Frances and Day stuff
Pompapom pompapom pimpapombimbam

Khaki's a nice quiet colour
Tin hats don't shine
Sombre as a Humphry Davy
In a fire-damp mine.

Soldiers, who form in double file
With a grave space between
Your gantry wants its cross shorings
With bayonets in.

Death in the spirit-level
Governs your double line
Khaki's a nice quiet colour
Tin hats don't shine...
Ben saying: 'Come boys – what's the odds, your khaki against
my dungarees', but they knocked him off before he got any
farther.

# In the Beginning: *A Broken Narrative*

I

The Study Circle often comes very
near to a deadlock.

Tonight's warped with the pull of streets about houses:
Bob pulls it one way – *Distance* as a Busdriver –
Alec the other, *Haste* the taximan
But engine-driver Jim will parcel up the town
To a word seen only if you look out sharp
Early or late? Just passed it. Dead on time.
And as he passes the houses tremble
And the tenants trembling inside them, and the street itself
Going up, going down.

Streets tautened about houses and houses about men's heads
Bob, Alec, Jim: Speed!
But Bert lamplighter came out very leisurely
Scouting for duds when the clockwork light's switched on.
(Jock down at the Power House, stoker having played a couple
of games at dominoes, the foreman conniving, gets back to his
taps, all lights on, night here, peak load)

Twilight a slow tune of debt between houses and men,
The light, the shade, the debt, the difference: How much?

An oblong space in a buff form
Number          street     town
Name    sex       date of birth
In the beginning was the word
Sixty minutes to the hour, but by the hour
How much?

We sit here explaining
Us        –        them      –        us.

Then Bill getting up – creak,
Bob moving where the sofa spring sticks out: crake
Jock putting a squashed face on it
And Bert – you could see his eye looking through streets and
any number of stone walls,
And as for Jim: would you say he looked or that things,
things, things, things, looked at him and he looked away?

We sit here explaining
But if one day May Day –
If this bus drew out of its road, 73 or 173
Banged across Oxford Street to break a cordon
If taxi drew out of its rank
Swung out at the bottom of the Euston inclined plane
Where steam sizzles under the low-eaved glass
Sizzles through a Euston of Manchester smoke,
Rugby, Stafford, Wigan, Oldham, Preston, Carnforth smoke
And heard Red Front and a whistle shouting
Jim on the footplate fist up in the salute
And the Power House a double pitched bellow
Town lights twice-flickered as a Jock signal: If –

II
It's no use just
swinging your
right: you've
got to connect.
Once was. General strike. '26.

Bob's voice laughs and lazy lingers abed
Bob's eye shut for a good long lie in
And a Churchill gazette getting it under his skin
With something about the community
The women and children
Murmuring like a voice half heard at the point of waking
(Nobody there)
Oozing like the long quiet days we had at sea
(said Bob and wondered).

No wheels in his hands
No taxi to spurt ahead as advance guard
No Power House to bellow
The locomotive in its shed

I ask the secretary (Bob said) how he thought it was going to
work out for the miners, & c.
But his mouth shut like a zip fastener.

In the beginning was the word. Huckster. How much?
Their countersign's *Debt-payment: Contract.* What's ours?
A lost secret?
Can it compound the tension?
Can it make men with empty hands the pivotal points they
were?
Give back the power and the glory?
The sirens, the engines, the 90 miles an hour speed?
In the beginning was –
Cut out the saint stuff, let's get down to business –
In the beginning was the deed.

III
the factory
and the
dinner-hour meeting.

Wood grain is tension which being released log splits. The boiler
with more accelerated molecule being red hot is splashed with cold
water and lo, a molecule opens its mouth like a ducked Hitler,
gasps with heart momentarily stopped, and a crack spreads.
A tension holding men together in this factory, over against a
field of fear, insulated by the indifferency of a larger field,
procured that clear direction of electric strain that lighted the
Fifth Light.

There were four lights, red, yellow, green and red,
Official flashes speaking to the machining shed.
First light said go. One went. Third light flashed and was answered,
Word became light in the machining shed.

There was also a Fifth Light nobody saw flicker
But it drove the charge-hands hither and thither.
A fifth light, a mystery, was there and was not there,
What colour was it flashing invisibly from nowhere?

The Fifth Light had for its element
A simple contrivance of terminals and filament.
Three men. One taking the current trembled.
The Fifth Light sent a word through the machining shed.

It was understood. Sufficed that it was understood to induce
power. Split the men, said the boss. Turn direction into
indirection. Atomise. So here's the scene.

'Workmates, I'm not up here of free will. You've seen the Fifth
Light, the rag that's sold to us at the gate by strangers. But it isn't
written by strangers. And the proof is it shouts your private
thoughts back at you.
'You're a fair-minded lot. You know I'm Labour and proud of it.

I've dealt straight with the masters.  They are, as they've made
us, copartners in a great concern. So for me this Fifth Light's
like a nightmare where somebody jerks your elbow.  And you
can't see who.
'Yesterday I was fetched to the office and asked if I had to do
with the Fifth Light. They said, "Either you get it stopped
or...we'll be sorry to lose you."
'I'm not going to come the sob-stuff. I know I'm sacked unless
one of you speaks up. I don't know who he is but I know he's
here. I want to know if he's going to have the guts to show
himself. Well? I'm going to wait for it.'

Canteen's a rest, canteen's a pause for working,
Colourful as a tank and as comfortable as a knifeboard,
And silent.
Has the deed become a word then,
And silence?

## IV

Come on the roof, dinner time's
nearly over.  Sky's high to-day.
Remember how the Soviet balloonists saw
the blue go black in the stratosphere?

The morning from the factory roof
Is glossy as a circus mare
And us like two weather-cocks
Buffeted and as bare.

Skies, violet in the early stage
Purple by increment,
Inaugurate the stratosphere
Black as bedazzlement:

Sun-bathing our defiances
Toughening skin to breed,
Dimitrov physiognomies
Like greyhounds are for speed.

\*\*\*

I cavilled: 'If we'd spoken up...'
Ben's answer was a grin,
Twitching hid face, and a word like a rivet
Red hot, to be dropped in.

# The Hunter and the Hunted

I was a Stoic philosopher
In the lonely days of youth
I studied every day and night
They told me I'd find truth
And wisdom when I learned enough
And goodness absolute.

I met a Cynic on the way
Who played the Socrates.
'In what way is the thing you seek
Different from happiness?'
He asked. It seemed as if I looked
Over a precipice.

I told him of my mentors and
The stoic's final goal:
To lose all fear, desire, regret
And anger never feel.
And then – I still recall his smile –
Scarcely do they feel at all.

And yet now I am older I
Regret those happy days
When not to seek was one way of
Discovering happiness.
Now it hunts me and therefore I
Understand tragedies.

# Where My Bones Rest

Number the snaky vertebrae
Into the central mattress thrust:
Raise a knee and plant a sole!
Now my bones rest.

And ceiling-contemplative lie
Draining away the sorry dust
From brain and spinal fluid: so I
And my bones rest.

Tail and scapula and skull
Digging hollows like the beasts
Scratching needed earthworks where
All our bones rest.

Pain has its pulse, is passionate,
The body stretched upon a cross
Of its old victories and defeats,
While my bones rest.

Count then the snaky vertebrae
Into the central mattress thrust:
And raise a knee and plant a sole,
And my bones rest.

# The Ambassador

Underneath the broad hat is the face of the Ambassador.
He rides on a white horse through Hell looking two ways.
Doors open before him and shut when he has passed.
He is master of the mysteries. And in the market place
He is known. He stole the trident, the girdle,
The sword, the sceptre and many mechanical instruments.
Thieves honour him. In the Underworld he rides carelessly.
Sometimes he rises into the air and flies silently.

# A Ballad from Korea

*Based on two newspaper correspondents' dispatches*

The password was Madison Square
That night the bugles sounded,
The Chinese bugles that declared
Our unit was surrounded
And the password was Madison Square.

The G.I.s had fallen back
From their part of the line
Leaving exposed our flank
So the Chinese closed in
And the password was Madison Square.

The Chinese knew the password
Their drummers beat tattoo
And 'Madison Square!' they shouted,
Gongs beating, they broke through
And the password was Madison Square.

They said to me, Bill Pongo,
These Chinese said to me
'There's your way home, Private Pongo
Go home and work for peace.'
The password is 'Work for Peace.'

'We have no war with working men,'
These Chinese said to me,
There's your way home, Private Pongo
Go home and work for peace,
The password is 'Work for Peace.'

The password Madison Square,
The password Work for Peace
If one of these is the right one
Which of them would you choose?

# Character Equals Situation

Character equals situation
I used to think, and think so yet:
But being older my condition
Places an emphasis on death
As the near limit.

The situation, then, is man,
Upright, so prone to hernia
Who in the transports of his joy
Emits premonitory fear.
This is his summit.

All situations we can count
(The learned mention thirty-six)
Are worth only a small amount –
Forged guarantee or syphilis.
The truth is richer.

Say to a playwright, 'Find a plot.'
He picks his fancy from the index
But Romeo and Juliet
At a building estate window
Feel, feel it's different.

They feel, and what they feel's the point.
The infinite has a finite sum
And works statistically out
But meanwhile the emotions come
Home to roost. Home.

'Colour comes home into the eyes'
And dreams invent mythology
A fabulous code made to deny
The plain man's plain prosaic lie,
His treachery which is shame.

# Exercise with a Broad Nib

Cudworth a Cambridge don
Made the discovery that man
Naturally knows good from evil
Though Eve had to be told by the devil.

Cudworth decided you've a feeler
(Watch it waver! Watch it waver!)
Touch will discover woman's beauty
But not, Jack, your duty.
Eyes will descry the infinite
But not what's right.
The ear discerns sonata form
Not indecorum.
The gusto that will sauce your dinner
Makes you a sinner
Nor shall the sharpness of your nose
Rival that other sense which knows
As datum – given –
What's what in heaven.

You have five sense? No there's one
More to come
Which Cudworth in his innocence
Called Common Sense.

And thus the triangle is eternal:
This common knowledge, being paternal,
Is transferred to the weaker vessel
Only by intercourse with the devil.

# Helen Was Not Up Was She

Helen of Troy said to Priam
Helen of Troy (she said)
If Paris fashions were my only passion
There'd be little more to be said
But there's sieges and wars and epics where I am
Wherever I show my head
Helen of Troy (she said)

Helen of Troy said to Priam
Helen of Troy she said
If you want to be king of the town where I am
The rage and the beauty (she said)
You may be king of the siege but I am
The lover's beloved (she said)
You may be Troy's great I am, Priam
But Helen's the wine and the song and the bread,
Helen of Troy (she said)

Helen of Troy said to Priam
Helen of Troy (she said)
The grave is deep but the tower is higher
Sky-reaching tower, she said
This is my city, the wall is what I am
Binding it all, she said
Here where I live, where I am, Priam
This is where I am (she said)
But Priam said nothing for this was the place where
Priam Priam was dead
Troy is burnt down (she said).

# Now Praise...

Now praise the twentieth century
That with long study
Has rediscovered
The human body

Which taking thought
On its own nature
Can add a cubit
To its structure.

Fatigue may cloud
The spinal fluid
But thought will speed
The dancing blood

Which traces veins
So delicate
That you would say
The body thought.

Bare to the sun
Worship and study
This gold, this golden
Human body.

# The Obituary

He lies in stiff dishonoured shroud
Who being offered it refused love
And, as he is now, was stiff.

He lies in his dishonoured shroud
Who being challenged thus was afraid,
His heart, small and still as it is now, dismayed.

He wore over his head
Fears and evasions like a hood
Which wrapped him round as now
The stiff dishonoured shroud.

# The Answer

Fear is an economy
Of spirit, and if he
Accepted, might it not be
True death (and this one is false – he sleeps?)

Is it not wise to say
If all my previous days
Lead to this end I may
Accept this love – if not I must deny?

Though to deny was stiff
And clammy on the lip
As a foretaste of death...
This judgement still ends in an 'if':
The indecision is the sign of life.

# The Pitfall

Too much or too little,
That is the pitfall,
Too much or too little,
Love.

Call it the wolf trap,
The gallows drop,
The hidden gap,
The grave.

Too much or too little
That is the pitfall.

Too much – her hand,
Naked and kind
Bridling Cupid's mind
Like her doves.

Too much or too little,
That is the pitfall.

But when there's too little
The childish lost soul
Dies in an infantile
Life.

Too much or too little,
That is the pitfall,
Too much or too little
Love.

# St Venus's Eve

There was a saint called Venus
Who rose out of the sea.
She has her saints' day like the rest,
This is St Venus Eve.
Tonight in every street
The pattering of feet
Says: 'Flower of the pine
You keep your morals and I'll keep mine.'

He who has never loved shall love tomorrow
Tomorrow the tired lover shall find love.

In her long winter absence
We know what we have lost –
But in her blessed presence
This knowledge we'd have missed.
Tonight in every street
The pattering of feet
Says: 'Flower of the quince
I let Lisa go and what good is life since?'

He who has never loved shall love tomorrow
Tomorrow the tired lover shall find love.

From this world's lack of love
Tomorrow's holiday.
The greater love the nearer death
Tomorrow we shall die.

Tonight in every street
The pattering of feet
Says: 'Flower of the peach
Death for us all and his own life for each.'

He who has never loved shall love tomorrow
Tomorrow the tired lover shall find sleep.

# A Sentence of Judges

Lawyers in their wigs divide
Right from wrong, their law's judge-made.
Ride her pilot as you can
Law shall decide which is the man.

Shoot a line for O you're brave
Tracing an invisible path!
Law with finer razor cut
Splits the hair and measures guilt.

Action? This is the act – the law,
This is what the rest was for,
Fighting and loving: this the last
Judgment is the only act.

Vainly you resist with logic
All its existential magic
For what judges is a past –
Denied – that swallows us at last.

Women in diaphanous veils
Lest your dream your power prevails:
General in cocks' feathers proud:
Lawyers in their wigs decide....

Unless in curious reversal,
And last minute bouleversement,
Essence ups and overturns
Existence heavy on the throne?

## The Spirit Kills

Spirit kills thought: the letter is for meaning –
For thought, like a neurotic in his moaning
Desires sweet tea, and definite moorings –
Facts to get teeth into – anything boring.

The spirit kills, the letter giveth life:
Spirit kills love, putting on oath
A cumulus of perjured evidence.
The spirit kills: the letter is concupiscence.

# To Chloe with an Old Valentine

Chloe, this piece of nonsense please
Interpret with a double-take
As meaning nearly what it says
For rather more than old time's sake.

Great passion, boasting it endows
Heirs of – for what it's worth – creation,
Will wring no envy out of us
For our love's in imagination

Arcadia where our better halves
Can meet in private fantasy:
Victorian, water-coloured selves,
Luckier than real you or me.

So, in this poem, edged with lace
For fluttered February's blind date
Read what it decorously says
But take it with a double-take.

# When I Awake

When I awake and count my sins
Before the dawn chorus begins
Swallowing dregs of cowardice
And defeat inflicted lies,
One sin there is no need to hide:
There's no self-punishment for pride.

Pride defeated and laid low
Has a heavy debt to pay:
Natural exacerbation
Concentrates upon the payment.
Loss of pride becomes the sin
Pride flows back when I'm forgiven.

So that striking balance I
Can regain complacency
Forgive o Lord the sin of pride
It is my necessary food,
Without which, surely, I would drop
Into the nothingness of sleep.

# Untitled

You are a stranger, one whose face
Seen casually in a public place
Puzzles me. Where did I before
See that brow and hear that talk –
Accents so free no doubt assails them –
And in your gestures see your children?

Not young, nor old, but much as I am,
In pride of life or else its doldrum
(About the pride you'd have no doubts:
Doldrums would be your partner's fault).
Bold flower we humbly breathe your pollen
And in your gestures see your children.

By them in time you'll be replaced
(And me they'll superannuate!)
No! Now I see your wisdom is
To turn their future into past
And dazzling their weak rebellion
Your lovely gesture keeps them children.

# Poems from an Ibo Sequence

*The largest tribe in Nigeria, the Ibos are not far removed from matriarchy: in their own proverb, 'The Ibo has no chiefs.' They inhabit the escarpment east of the Niger.*

## I: Iboland

It has the shape of a far distant country,
Farther than innocence, as far
As wisdom: Ibo women wear
Breasts painted as a sign they are
Wives, mothers, ancient queens accounted.

This one was old. Her feet and breasts were leather.
The dreamy boy she stood beside
Wrote for her in his schoolboy style
A plaintive letter full of guile
Calling a distant son to come and save her.

And I said, 'Let me go your way,'
Being curious to see her home.
The village laughed to see us come
Shouting 'Hey ma, you're past your time!'
I saw her enemies glowering neighbourly

And knew that I was here in Iboland,
Here where the evil bush is sad
Because it mutters my own mind,
And Conscience, an albino, pads
Naked behind the others with his load.

## II: A Dark Place Under the Trees

A dark place under the trees
Is called a town though there is nothing to see
Beyond the darkness under the trees.

A pale goat runs from the dark place,
Its flesh almost white, a hornless face –
As if a nightmare bred a giant mouse.

Emerging with a cheerful bound
A mongrel leaves the so-called town.
What miscegenation made this stunted hound?

A homelier apparition follows:
A laying hen with flying feathers,
So small a bantam would be jealous.

A young girl with pouting breasts
And protruding umbilicus
Dives back into a shadowy place.

It is all there if you could see,
What lunacy longs for and fears,
A dark place under the trees.

## III: This is Our Love Child

'This is our love child.' If the phrase
Were spoken in a theatrical voice
Throbbing to admit disgrace
This is the opposite of the way
These lovers said it,
Standing in the criss-cross paths
There in the town bush burning with
Africa's intemperate rays,
'This is our love child.'

'This is our love child.' Naked, bold,
With the aplomb of one year old
She stretched a hand for each to hold
Displaying in the childish folds
Of her neck corals:
Her father a slim, naked youth
Jock-strapped and bearded: mother's cloth
Was brown as her firm breasts above.
'This is our love child.'

And I, being white, petitioned to
As if a magistrate or an Ozo
By these three Ibos, kneeling down
Under a palm in the bush town
Heard a translation:
'Because my husband has refused
The sum he gave as my bride price
Our love child legally is his.'
Thus their petition:

'Pray, sir, compel her husband take
Repayment of the price he gave
And thus divorcing let her leave.'
The lover's square beard jutted brave
The love-child swelled its chest
While Daniel, fat interpreter
Behind me with my retinue
Lavished some pints of sweat into
His cotton vest.

The love child waited: there we stood
In the deep Chuku-haunted wood
And money spread a solemn shade
The bride price was a wedding veil.
The love child too
Will soon be worth what she can fetch,
When puberty distends her breasts
Her legal father will collect
Her bride price too.

## IV: Men and Women Almost Equal

Men and women almost equal
In Iboland
Feel their way towards the inevitable
Indecision of the sequel.

The women are gentle, their so-called masters
Are husbandmen of the smaller harvest:
But change brings force and force brings menace.

Masculinity becomes
Acid in the ancient homes.
(Masculine is the imagination
Also in Iboland.)

Cruelty begets despair
Women's gentleness disappears
And astonished children wail

Whipped with flexible stinging canes
In the tin-shack streets of Lagos –
New world, new ways, new dispensation.

It is the vain longing for the bush
The dark place under the trees and rest
On the millionfold black breasts
Of Iboland.

# On a 17th Century Painting

A daylight fire springs from a dying furze
A too obedient Abraham turns back
Eyeing his son as Phaedra shall eye hers
And the sky cringes to the thunder clap:

And then the deluge, if hysteria dare
Tempt the sky's passion with a wanton show
Of exaltation in the womb of air.
Last, in a general promise, comes the bow.

# Royal Academy: Special Exhibition

Gala concert, Filarmonic, Venice (1782)
Painted at his easy best by clever Guardi (Francesco)
Sets the human problem squarely. Here the audience is sat down
Under the high-vaulted marble and the wine is passing round:
Violins, perched on a ledge, the musicians' gallery:
Behind them stand the women singers in respectful symmetry
While the candelabras glitter, fashionable shoulders gleam—
Individuals merged in audience waiting the composer's theme...
Many centuries are piled to make this velvet finery:
Guardi's highlights and his glazes now provide us with a key
To another kind of music. We owe a debt of gratitude
To Guardi for his architectural painting of 1782.

Next door are the earlier panels: Christ is mocked, a virgin born
Mars strips Venus, and Giotti's golden skies are Byzantine;
And the individual feeling that his questing ego's gone
In among these splendid visions finds his ego not alone:
We create our gods and angels, we create ourselves, and then
Out of ribs create a lover out of sympathies a friend.

Guardi's concert, Filarmonic, Venice 1782
Takes a reading in his sextant of a different latitude.
All the finery, the ribbons, the gilt chairs are comme il faut
Certainly du monde is present but no individual soul
Not a pair of lovers, nor a torturer, nor Mars
Nor Giotto to encircle warmth with his Byzantine skies.
There is neither history nor suffering: it is all
Horeshair scraping over catgut and vibrating vocal chords
Candelabra and the velvet touched to highlights with a glaze
Clever Guardi learned the trick of in his architectural days.

Can you smell the smell of order which has neither ears nor nose
Only odour of the odour of these bodies without pores?
Music cannot reach them therefore nor can sweat nor can the ardour
That might tempt to good or evil or the apple in the garden.
We've no people here but figures ranged according to a plan,
Guardi knew it, Guardi saw it, Guardi, he's your man:
Points of light and points of darkness. Darkness, darkness which endures
From 1782 to 19... My guess is as good as yours.

# Your Touch Has Still

Your touch has still its ancient power,
Painter, and your full brush has made
Mythology of old desire
New.  The explorer is afraid.

Violence and crime and lingering death,
And love forced on unwilling limbs,
The sunshiny agony of the flesh –
Your touch sets to familiar hymns.

Your god is carried to the tomb,
The bearers straining at the slings
Under the loins. Canvas shows through
Where the work is unfulfilled.

Mythology breaks down, a gap
Lets in the undecided hope.
Your touch has still its power perhaps
Also in knowing where to stop.

Your touch has still its ancient power
For man imagining a form in which
Eager and feminine desire
Is given lastingness in myth.

## Past Years

Past years brood on the plain like painted clouds
Which never can move into afternoon.
I shall not today be roused as I was once roused
By riddles and ballads sung to a folk tune.

These were my children of serenity
They told me secrets and they gave me power
But now their shadows in vain haunt me
In sunset mystery, the twilight hour.

To call a sound from past and quiet seasons –
Create a soul trembling with life at last –
In vain my crooked fingers pluck the harp.

Lost now is youth, and lost its far horizons
Mute in my throat the tunes of the rich past.
Shadows are round my feet and it is dark.

# Part II

# Songs and Choruses from Dramatic Works

# Ballad

Listen to the mournful drums of a strange funeral,
Listen to the story of a strange American funeral.

In Braddock Pennsylvania
Where the steel mills flare
The spring came in like a frightened child
In an ogre's lair.

Jan Clepak a Bohemian
Going to work at five
Sees grass on the hills across the river
Plum blossoms all alive.

He sweats at his pudding trough
Half-naked like a fiend
And the blossoming memories soften his heart
Make his thoughts mild

He thinks of cows and sheep
In sunny Bohemia
And his baby's little laughters and the way men sing
When they're happy and drunk.

Listen to the mournful drums of a strange funeral,
Listen to the story of a strange American funeral.

Wake up brother Clepak, wake up
Wake up, it's ten o'clock
The furnaces roar and the mad flowing steel
Pours into your puddling trough.

Wake up, the lever's cracked
The steel is running through
Wake up! Oh, the dream is ended, the steel has got you.
Jan Clepak's napoo.

Three tons of hardened steel
Hold at their heart and bones
The nerves, the muscle of Jan Clepak
And his dreams of home.

The steel mill directors
A coffin of steel will give
To the widow and the family of the late Jan Clepak
To go in a giant grave.

His widow and two friends
Ride in a carriage behind
The truck with the three ton of block steel
With Jan Clepak inside.

Listen to the mournful drums of a strange funeral,
Listen to the story of a strange American funeral.

By the grave one thinks to himself
'I shall never get drunk from now on
Nor ever get married for life is a dirty
Joke like Jan's funeral.'

'I'll wash clothes, scrub floors,
I'll be fifty per cent tart
But my kids won't work in the steel mill'
Says his wife in her heart.

'I'll make myself as hard as steel, harder,
Like bullets from Jan's corpse',
The other friend's thinking, listening,
What to? Drums of course.

# Speech for a Fascist

Men, comrades, now that you are going to enter
A night of fear and a winter of war
Does it seem good that we should go over
What is our cause, what our convictions are?

You know, most of you, how the Marxists
Sprinkle desire with a dry sand,
Till women's beauty and man's physical courage
Are sick with self-distrust and undermined.

You know, most of you, how the Jew in business
Has turned virtue into advertisement,
Buying and selling love; and that the Freemasons
Have made kingliness into a cheap scent.

You know we promise no millennium.
Whatever reward there is, is in the fight.
We warn you that it may not prove possible
To set mankind's twisted reactions right.

We offer you, simply the opportunity
To free your daydreams from the mirror's ghost
And free your hate – for when hate is secreted
Man's blood is poisoned and his seed is lost.

Beware of him who has no vices
There are less innocent forms of power.
We hail the dignity of laying down
Our old self-worship in our country's hour.

We shall not hide war and its bitterness.
We tell this lost battalion that its weird
Is air attack and treacherous poison warfare.
This, our Golgotha, is to free the world.

And lead mankind into a sunlight fighting,
Corpuscles flushed and lungs full of fresh air
And clean quarrels and new adventures –
Life as it was before the Jew was there!

\*\*\*

You know that death and torture are our weapons
Sup full of horrors. When you feel
The steel whip on your hide, then you know our lessons
Are rudimentary but they are not dull.

# Chorus from *Easter 1916*

| | |
|---|---|
| Woman | Is Pity abhorrent? |
| Man | Is Pity a tyrant |
| | When bombs, explosions |
| | Mark her decisions? |
| Woman | Sure bullets quiver |
| | And shriek whenever |
| | The warm flesh stops them. |
| Man | Our sandbags trap them. |
| Woman | Your thoughts are bullets |
| | And hearts their targets. |
| Man | Your pity's a tremor |
| | Soldiers allow for |
| | In every manoeuvre. |
| Woman | Until they meet |
| | Their own death in the street |
| | And swift bereavement |
| | On the white pavement. |
| Man | Your pity weakens |
| | Hope when it quickens. |
| Woman | Hope's no more needed |
| | We'll sacrifice it: |
| | But leave us the lovers |
| | For whom we prize it. |
| | Leave shillings to spend |
| | And pennies to keep |
| | And the warm featherbed |
| | Of sleep. |
| Man | Sleep is a death that |
| | Waking to combat |
| | Thrusts a cold nozzle |
| | Into the snuggle. |
| Woman | Your thoughts are bullets. |
| Man | And men their targets. |
| Woman | What wrong have they done you? |
| Man | Their minds are without hope. |

## Mother Comfort:
## a Song for Two Female Voices

Dear, shall we talk or will that cloud the sky?
Will you be Mother Comfort or shall I?
If I should love him where would our lives be?
And if you turn him out at last, then friendship pity me.
My longing like my heart, beats to and fro
Oh that a single life could be both Yes and No.
Will you be Mother Comfort or shall I?
Ashamed to grant and frightened to refuse
Pity has chosen, Power has still to choose.
But darling, when that stretched out will is tired
Surely your timid prettiness longs to be over-power'd?
Sure gossips have this sweet facility
To tell transparent lies and, without pain, to cry.
Will you be Mother Comfort or shall I be Mother Comfort?
Will you be Mother Comfort or shall I?

# Chorus from *Stay Down Miner*

| | |
|---|---|
| Man | Time, in the shape of a mine, time in that shape |
| | Has the same backward progress underground, |
| | And past explosions are now lighted roads. |
| | Then turn away from lights and trams and whitewash |
| | Into the critical *Present* where workings narrow: |
| | Bend double at the coal-face, bend double and approach |
| | The blank wall of the future. |
| Woman | Pit-prop carefully behind you, |
| | Pit-prop and scatter stonedust. |
| Man | Time in the shape of a mine – |
| Woman | Can you go on now? |
| Man | Whether with pneumatic drill shattering eardrums |
| | Or whether the mechanical cutter hauls |
| | Its great bulk into the underface like a tank, |
| | Or whether, after your drilling, the charge of dynamite |
| | Implies 'stand back' and the fireman's signal |
| | And thunder blasting unknown addition to |
| | Time, in the shape of a mine, stretching back... |
| Woman | Stretching back, maybe, this time with |
| | A fallen rock between you and the world |
| | (Two or three cut off) and a rescue party |
| | Tapping at the other end of the solid. |
| Man | Sound travels. You can hear through solidity. |
| Woman | And die in the dark hearing. Then it is finished |
| | Miner's knowledge and his skull cracked |
| | Instantaneously... Time in the shape of a miner |
| | Left for dead in the workings. |
| Man | Another time along main haulage roads |
| | Past conveyors, trams, electric lights |
| | Comes fire, flood chaos and general death. |
| | One thrust at the future brought that mighty death. |
| Woman | Time in the shape of a mine is three dead every day. |
| | It is the shape of time, one thousand and seventy-three in a year. |
| Man | We have our roundabout apart from yours, |

Twenty-four hours divided into shifts.
Your marriages, your pregnancies and deliveries
By district nurses hurrying on bicycles,
Your shops, your credits, have no obvious harmony
With this dark round of ours, this onward march
Of Time along with death and fire and flood
And speed against time weighing coal we get;
This nice precision of the hewer's path,
This separate world; this pit; this underground,
Time, caring little for the upper crust.

Woman  Have you got new men (otherwise we are lost)
Have you got new men, themselves shaping
Time in the shape of their knowledge of necessity,

shaping

Time according to the seam, according to geology,
Time for man, not man for Time,
Time for man! Time for man!
Have you got new men (otherwise we are lost)
And mines will feed on men as wars do
Have you got new men to fight this other time?
New men, new men to overcome it, till
Time, in the shape of a mine, is the equation
Of an enriching life!

Man  Yes. We have new men.
The new man, here, now, braving novel death,
Stands upright in the mine, and in that posture
Shakes more than pit-props.

# Deleted Song from *Stay Down Miner*

These foothills which we speak of as a mountain
Are crossed by long-legged sheep and telpher span.
Mountains are formed by turmoil in earth's crust;
The minerals bear their backs and miners must.

If any peak, however weather-worn
Feels dental-drillings, then a town is born:
Sometimes unsheltered, where the bracken grew
And sometimes pouched as by a kangaroo.

The foothills splayed like fingers on a hand
Shelter the southern ports and fatter land;
Oh! Climb still northward where the wrist joins on
To the Black Mountains and the hills of Brecon.

Oh! Climb still northward and against the wind
Into a world of mineral-bearing ground.
Mountains are formed by turmoil in the earth's crust;
The minerals bear their backs and miners must.

# Chorus (from an unidentified pageant)

O in this spring-tide you would say the sun
Had been drowned also, and that one by one
The waves wash over it, and the waves shout
With the diffused glory that they toss about.

Turn from the tide, the tide that overflows
Wind-laden, for its murmuring power will blow
Tonight into a storm that calendars
Will boast and marvel at in coming years.

# Chorus from 'Towards Tomorrow' (1938)

We are women. Is to weep
The last privilege we keep?
We are women and we bore
All the fighters in your war

Men you mustered into hell
While our daughters filled the shells
That scattered villages in dust,
And rags and sticks and flesh that rots.

We are women; and the curse
Of plague is given us to nurse.
We are women. Shall we keep
Women's custom still, and weep?

We whose sons and lovers were
Charred and maimed, disfigured there;
We whose lives of empty waiting
Losing hope are soured with hatred –

Shall we forgive with cheeks aglow
Hearing a mournful bugle blow?
Shall a leader terrorise
Us to see through coward's eyes?

We are women and we know
Flushed cheek and fever glow,
And the music crying glory,
And the ancient lying story.

We are women and we know
How much fighting is to do;
How much blood to make a dawn;
With what pangs a man is born.

We are women and we know
Knives are wanted to cut free.
If a priest leads to the grave
Woman still leads back to life.

We are women, shall we keep
Woman's custom still, and weep?
Or take life and love in hand
Love for this or any land

For the children gazing now
Into vistas of dismay
For the gardens that will gape
Into shelter pits and graves

Women who have suffered long
Stand unarmed against the strong
Know the enemy is down
When his heart is turned to stone

Our bare heads against this terror;
Our clear truth against this error,
Against his bowing down to death
The burning of our flame of life.

Now proclaim this day to gather
All the friends of life together
Siege the monster in his lair
Suffocate the god of war.

We are women and proclaim
This is the accepted time.
Nations, peoples, men and women
Children in the glow of morning

Make a ring around the aggressor
Dispossess the dispossessor
Build the warm alliances
Of humanity for peace.

# Chorus from 'An Agreement of the People' (1942)

...Civilisation, as they said,
Is either living or is dead
And the past mastery survives
As retranslated in our lives.

Behind success in battle lies
Eagerness searching in the skies
Exploring in the stratosphere
The long watch through the Polar Year
Devising aeroplanes on skis
To land on airfields made of ice
Wresting the secrets Nature hugs
And fights over like tiger cubs.
That is the cost. Experiment
Ever watchful where it went,
Aware if Nature shows no quarter
The human foe's an uglier master.

# A Verse for Arthur Benjamin

Spilt wine of blossom fallen from
The bitter almond tree
Brings like the red of autumn leaves
Past happiness to me.
This was the past: the petals fall
The sun has filled their veins.
Let it be now! Love's kingdom come.
O it is now he reigns,
O it is now love reigns!

# Part III
## Libretti and Poetic Dramas

# The Seven Ages of Man

The characters:
Man (40)
Infant (2)
Stepmother (30)
Fat woman (50), mother of
Girl (25)
Youth (18)
Grandad (80)

*The yard of a workman's cottage. On the left a sunflower, on the right, in the distance, a mill chimney. The man is discovered sitting, the infant staggering.*

Man        Says Joan t'owd man on a hot Friday night
        Tha mun go into't yard and mind thi own brat.
        If thou had to work as heavy as me
        Tha'd know why tha says I age faster'n thee.
        So t'owd man he sat on his bum with his brat
        And says, Let's have a good think.

        There's cheatin in life: when man's brisk in his day
        T'owd woman for spite begins to decay –

        *As the child falls.*

        Nay lad, shut up, tha's come to no harm
        Now shut thi row and I'll tell thee a yarn.
        Tha feels a bit dull when tha plays by thisel.
        ... Eh, thinkin's for them as as wealth.
        *He sings rocking the child in his arms*
        Tha's welcome here thou bonny brid
        But shouldn't ha come when tha did
        Times are bad
        But that o'course tha didn't know,
        So hunch up close, I'll help thee grow
        I'm thi dad.

I've often heard me father tell
As when I came int' world myself
Trade were slack.
Tha knows it's hard work pullin through
But I wean't scare thee. If I do
Tha'll go back.

*The infant is asleep. An outbreak of quarrelling wakes him.*

Now such a clatter comes about
One missis chasing t'other out.

*Enter stepmother followed by fat woman, both shouting.*

Man            *(to Stepmother)*
               It's thy barn as I've put to sleep.
Stepmother     And thine 'ud make pawnbroker weep –
               Comes home wi no rent – all't money spent,
               Blewed it on wench next door.

               You Mrs Black!
Fat woman      You Mrs White!
Stepmother     Thou should be shamed
Fat woman      I'm that all right
               If you're my partner.
Stepmother     Your daughter wean't.
               She's old enough to be his aunt!
               Seducin children!
Fat woman      Found in't midden!
Man            Tak barn and send lad here.
Stepmother     Nay that I'll not. I'll see him mon
               Or ye'll egg yananither on.
Fat woman      As soon be a slut as a naggin wife.
Stepmother     Ay? Jealous since tha's botched thi life.
Fat woman      Tha's a sweet liar.
Stepmother     Tha's a hoor.

*The man gives her the child to handicap her exuberance.*

Man            Nay tak brat. He's got to learn.

*Exeunt stepmother with infant, followed by fat woman. Music. The girl comes in. The man does not turn round at first. After two of a dance he sees her.*

| | |
|---|---|
| Man | What's doin here? |
| Girl | Come to see thee. |
| Man | Thou? |
| Girl | Ay. |
| Man | Come to see me? |
| | Is it about yon lad? |
| Girl | About thisel. |
| Man | If I weren't wed already ye'd do very well. |
| | Tha's young lass. |
| Girl | Aye, and the years go by |
| | And I nivver find yan good enough. |
| Man | Nay lass thou – is a good lookin lass |
| | There's mony a lad would turn out his brass |
| | And tie himself up for the look o thy feace |
| Girl | I'm twenty-four and I ne'er had a kuss. |
| Man | Tha's a fibber lass. |
| Girl | Nay. |
| Man | Ne'er a one in play? |
| Girl | Ay, laakin but that doesn't count. |
| Man | Eh lass I'm a mon o past thirty-eight |
| | And well nigh settled in't married state. |
| | Tha mustn't tempt me. |
| Girl | What's tha mean by tempt? |
| | I'm nobbut conversin wi thee like a friend. |
| Man | Tha knows lass in't ageing the fire is raging |
| | The more cos it's soon to be quenched. |
| Girl | *(Breaks into the song)* |
| | Then the little maid she said, your fire may warm the bed |
| | But what shall we do for to eat? |
| | Will the flames you're only rich in, light a fire in the kitchen |
| | Or the little god of love turn the spit? |
| Man | That's a song and a bit. |
| Girl | It's a nursery rhyme, |
| Man | T'young uns don't twig what they miss at the time. |
| | Gie us a dance. |
| Girl | A clog dance! |

| | |
|---|---|
| Man | Nay. |
| | Clogs were for work and tha's for play. |
| Girl | *(dancing)* What if thi son should see us now? |
| Man | Dance on lass and shut thi row. |
| Girl | What if my mother come? |
| Man | Dance on. |
| | Tha's safer at dancin than some. |

*The son enters. The dance stops awkwardly.*

| | |
|---|---|
| Man | Eh lad? Tha knaws we're only laakin. |
| Son | I know folks sing when they don't like speakin. |

*As the girl turns.*

| | |
|---|---|
| | Thee? |
| Girl | Thou peepin – ! |
| Son | Call me that... |
| Girl | Nay but I called thi nothin yet. |
| Son | Wilta get out? |
| Girl | With thee about |
| | I'd best be o't way. |

*The girl goes. The boy remains.*

| | |
|---|---|
| Man | Nay lad, there isna need to cry. |
| Boy | Who's cryin then? |
| Man | Tha's got a weak eye. |
| Boy | Tha's got a weak brain. |
| Man | It's my moral sense |
| | Exhausted wi countin my shillings and pence. |
| | She's a bitch lad, and thou – too young for to know |
| | How complicate beauties are made. |
| Boy | When I was a kid I cried for the moon. |
| | Now I know I cried too soon. |
| | It's not the moon you ought to wail for |
| | But lack in yourself and your own failure. |
| | You look in the glass and see your own face – |
| | And keep your tears to yourself. |
| Man | Nay lad, what's all this onyway? |
| | Lad, there's a peck o good in thee. |
| | When green melancholy comes |

|       | Nay lad nay – stick up thi thumbs! |
|-------|-------------------------------------|
|       | For tha's got the looks, and tha's got the guts |
|       | To win thiself owt that thi wants. |
| Boy   | Owt I want? What's that? If ever I knew |
|       | What I want I'd know what to do. |
|       | I still hold back and the twilight fetches |
|       | A longing for love and a fear of the wenches. |
| Man   | Hang on to yourself, it'll all come out well – |
|       | Tha's in love but tha don't know with who. |
| Boy   | I'm eighteen and time goes so quickly for me |
|       | I'm off down to Liverpool, going to sea. |
|       | I'll find out the world. Here nobbut a slave |
|       | I'll be sacked when I qualify for a man's wage. |
| Man   | Nay lad, tha naws, as nobody goes |
|       | To sea for adventure these days. |

Nay lad, all that drinking and swearing and thinking
Excited your blood till you're sweating and blinking.
Nay lad, cool thee down now, come whistle wi me
As 'I care for nowt and the dule cares for me.'
We whistle and grizzle, we fry and we frizzle Eh lad –
and then we grow up.

*The boy begins to do physical jerks that develop into a dance.*

That's it lad, that's it lad, get muscled and warm
In time tha'll be glad for the strength of thi arm.
Eh youth is a time of slackening and tightening,
It's still a game, still a game, when comes to fighting.

*The stepmother has entered unobserved.*

| Stepmother | And John Thomas Smith, if tha wean't come to grief |
|------------|--------------------------------------------------|
|            | Tha'll pack up and put thi to bed. |

*The boy goes out when he sees her. She makes as if to follow.*

| Man   | Owd woman art going? These neets are still growing |
|-------|---------------------------------------------------|
|       | So warm and so long, if tha stays I'll be showing |
|       | Thee how to find Orion, Plough and North Star |
|       | Milky Way and yon Pleiads, where they all are. · |
| Woman | I'd be a fool master to take thee for a schoolmaster |

If tha's sense tha'll come up to bed.

*The woman goes and he calls after her.*

Man    Owd woman art going, the neets are still growin
      So warm and so long, if tha stays I'll be showing

*The girl re-enters*

      Thee how to find Orion, Plough and North Star
      Milky Way and yon Pleiads, where they all are.
Girl     *(behind him)*
      I'm waiting to hear thee make it all clear
      For I can see nowt but a moon.
Man    Tha's a disturbing influence.
Girl     Tha'll go to bed if tha's got any sense.
Man    If I haven't what then?
Girl     Tha'll sing me a song.
Man    The second to-neet?
Girl     It needn't be long.
Man    Sing to't moon?
Girl     It'll keep thee in tune.
Man    And after that?
Girl     Maybe we'll see.
Man    *(sings)* There was a lad from out of Rochdale
      Whose face made film stars discontented
      Took out Bob's wife to tell the tale
      And when he whispered she consented.
      But to be short
      As these songs ought
      He used her well when he came with her
      And played his part with such an art
      She could not keep her lips together.

      When her husband he heard tell
      Of her tricks from her relations
      He would grumble to himself
      Very sad, in such a fashion
      Saying 'I'd give twenty pound
      That's ten more than I had with her
      If her ma would take her back

And make her keep her lips together.'

*During the song the fat woman has come in behind and surprises them.*

Fat woman    Ay? If them's the sort of songs
             Tha sings to this yan, tha belongs
             Yonder wi't second wife my friend.
Man          Nay, nay old woman, tha'll unbend
             Thisel for once, then tha'll ha sense.
Fat woman    Summat breaks whenever I bend.

             Mister, tha's got a pretty barn.
Man          What's that to thee, three ton o' charm?
Fat woman    Nowt. And tha'd a first wife too
             As gave thee a lad as is eighteen now.
             Tha's a busy mon.
Man          Ay. I like to get on.
Fat woman    Ay? At some other's expense.

             If thou and I had a drink together
             That would be more the kind o' weather
             For old uns like us.
Man          Eh speak for yoursel.
Fat woman    Ay I do that, an I drink very well
             I've known myself laugh for an hour and a half
             But I never did that before fifty.

             Nay lad, tha's too worried.
Man          Me worried?
Fat woman    Ay
             I see it all in thi worried blue eye.
             Tha's like bakin powder eatin its way
             Through flour till it's riz.

*The girl tiptoes out.*

Man          If tha has to say
             Any more o that sort I'll take thee to court.
Fat woman    Nay lad thou'll but join in and laugh.

See t'lass has gone home. Her sense is to come
She'll get in bed wi first barn.
At first she'll grow thinner wi barn drinking
dinner –
After fourth she'll grow fat and laugh.

An I can see in front o't moon
Thi daft old grandad has come down
I'm off cos t'owd man's silly talking
Shrivels me flesh and stops me laughing.
Thi grandad's coming, coming now,
Good neet lad, bed time for us a'.

*Exit Fat woman, enter Grandad.*

| | |
|---|---|
| Man | What is it grandad? Has't new moon |
| | Waked thee out o bed too soon? |
| | Or asta never been in p'raps |
| | Sat all neet mumblin at thi chaps? |
| Grandad | *(chanting)* Boys and girls come out to play |
| | T'moon is shining bright as day |
| Man | Nay grandad – eh – what is it now? |
| Grandad | Leave you supper, leave your sleep |
| | Join your playmates in the street. |
| Man | Grandad come and sit by me |
| Grandad | In the madness of the moon |
| | Playmates of the second noon |
| | Meet your rival in your shoes |
| | By the mirror introduced. |

One in bed and fast asleep
While the other in the street
(The moon sweating hot as day)
Supperless is tired of play.

| | |
|---|---|
| Man | Tha's a wise man grandad, tha's read books, |
| | Tha seest cause wherever tha looks. |
| | Tell me grandad dosta know why |
| | Men get moidered by t'moon in't sky? |
| Grandad | Because it's dead lad and it stays, |
| | Because a ghost's a mirror face. |

Boys and girls come out to play
T'moon is shining bright as day
Leave you supper, leave your sleep
Join your playmates in the street.

*A song is heard, off*

Singers All in this pleasant morning together come are we
    For summer springs so fresh green gay
    We'll tell you of a blossom that buds on every tree
    Drawing near to this morning of May.

Grandad Yon's t' May carol singers.

Man   Nay. It's wireless.

*Song off continues*

Singers *(off)* Rise up the mistress of this house, your babe
     upon your breast
    For summer springs so fresh green gay
    And if your body be asleep we hope your soul has rest
    Drawing near to this morning of May.
    Rise up your little children and stand all in a row
    For summer springs so fresh green gay
    We should have called you one by one but your names
     we do not know
    Drawing near to this morning of May.
    Rise up the fair maid and of this house put on your gay
     attire
    For summer springs so fresh green gay
    And bring us out a can of beer and we'll sing an octave
     higher
    Drawing near to this morning of May

    So now we're going to leave you in peace and plenty
     here
    For summer springs so fresh green gay
    We shall not sing you May again until another year
    For to draw these cold winters away.

Another You have been listening to The Northern Tradition
voice  in the Regional Programme.

Man   Sitha grandad there's summat to beat

You and me settin in't yard th'whole neet.
Ant' moon comes up and t'moon goes down
And now it's day and work's to be done.

*Sirens begin to blow and the boy, the girl, the fat woman cross on their way to work.*

| | |
|---|---|
| Boy | T'moon comes up and t'moon goes down |
| | And sirens blow and work's to be done. |
| | And why they call this blinkin thing |
| | A siren's because of the tune it sings. |
| Girl | Come to me and be at rest |
| | And if you come you'll likely be lost. |
| Fat woman | These are sirens because they call. |
| | Men and women into the mill. |
| Man | Men and women and children – eh |
| | Tha sees nowt else, and every day |
| | Sirens play the same old tunes |
| | Men grow backwards, women have barns. |

*They have all gone to work. Grandad goes into the house.*

**CURTAIN**

# Old Spain

*A young man is asleep. Three kneeling women are his dream. They are in black, and in his dream they are calling to him from an invaded country.*

Man
If Matthew, Mark, Luke and John
Blessed the bed that I lie on;
If four angels round my bed
Came to mind my dreaming head –
Should I sleep sounder? But I know
There are no angels. Must I go?

1st woman
We mourn dead children first.
That dying hurts us most.

2nd woman
It is too late now to begin
Begetting or bearing again.

3rd woman
Calm, her son dying, one said, 'I
Am alive pointlessly.'

1st woman
If a lover is snatched away
A woman says, 'Do I live so bodily
That it matters?'

2nd woman
Yes.
She loses interest in days.

3rd woman
If you dare not understand
Pain as an invaded land
Let it be transfigured
To your own finger.
Think of Spain as the limit of
Your private love.

1st woman
In love hell
Is the impossible.

2nd woman
Death, not life makes
The bars of our cage.

Man
My loves and projects fail
Shall I bring loss to your aid?

1st woman
Our lives and our former peace
Were stuff for anxieties.

| | |
|---|---|
| 2nd woman | Our lives and our peace |
| | Though they were bitterness |
| | Though our dancers elect |
| | To dance in black, |
| All | Though ours were joys crossed out |
| | They are prisoned and caged about. |
| | We are caged in death. |
| | Bring knives to free us with. |
| 1st woman | Old Spain has held us |
| | Buried in histories, |
| 2nd woman | An arid past. |
| 3rd woman | A desert to cross. |
| 1st woman | Now you shall hear in England |
| | Old Spain... comes to an end. |

*The three sing.*

> Cortes when he left Old Spain
> Wanted golden ornaments
> Aztec treasures for the vain
> Women who're his worst expense.
> Cortes put crosses on the high
> Temples. He came home to die.
> ... Old Spain, Cortes
> Back to Old Spain to die.
>
> Cortes drove the Indians out
> From the Aztec city of Mexico
> Three days the exodus filled the streets,
> Dead and dying, and the queue was slow.
> And death and Cortes in the evening
> Held High Mass for the slaughtered heathen.
> ... Old Spain, Cortes
> Calls you back home to die.
>
> He went to school in Salamanca
> An indigent adventurer,
> And, orthodox, a true believer
> Converted men by massacre:
> Put Christ above the Aztec devil
> And died contemptibly in Seville.

|            | ... Old Spain, Cortes, |
|            | Back to Old Spain to die. |
| Man        | I had a friend went there |
|            | As an adventurer |
|            | Crying, 'New tobacco, new wine |
|            | New way with women.' |
| 1st woman  | And I pray he found |
|            | These to his own mind. |
| Man        | Another had waited |
|            | Many years for it |
|            | Refusing to touch |
|            | The rest of us |
|            | As latitudinarian. |
|            | We called him sectarian |
|            | Inhuman and abstract, |
|            | Too human and not |
|            | English enough yet. |
|            | But he had waited |
|            | Many years for it |
|            | Then he was ready |
|            | With one more body |
|            | Saw all history |
|            | Fulfilled in his gesture. |
| 2nd woman  | A revolutionary |
|            | Has a duty to die. |
| 1st woman  | The many carpenters |
|            | Miners and builders |
|            | Who saw this the natural |
|            | Stretch of the struggle: |
|            | Did you know any? |
| Man        | I knew one |
|            | Relentlessly driven on. |
|            | He had excuses. |
|            | They were uprooted. |
|            | His English life |
|            | Turned sour in his mouth. |
|            | The more frightened |
|            | The more tautened |

                    Something not him
                    Below his will.
                    He thought he was going to death,
                    Back safe knew this not enough,
                    Said, 'I go back
                    To my scheduled task.'
                    One asked him, 'Are you persuaded
                    This is not perverted
                    Like dipsomaniacs
                    Flying Atlantics?'
                    But his slow grin
                    Damped the question down.
Women               The news of him.
Man                 Such never come home.

*The Man sings.*

                    I, haunted by my dead
                    Refulgent friends
                    Find starting up in bed
                    That it was I who screamed.
Women               Our life has its own dawn.
Man                 In my complacency
                    Sleep has to be a league
                    Between deceivers, my presence
                    Here is an intrigue.
Women               Our life has its own dawn.

*The women sing and during the song the Man stretches out and his sleep becomes dreamless.*

Women               Our life accepts its dawn, and in
                    Accepting finds its will,
                    Like women sweeter for the risk,
                    Held by its love until,
                    Glad for the sloughing of the husk
                    It bears the grinding of the ear
                    Accepts the birth pangs that begin
                    Rending the belly till a child is born.
                    Death had a festival but birth is here.
                    Our life accepts its dawn.

# Peter Grimes

**The Characters**

Peter Grimes, a fisherman
Boy, his apprentice
Ellen Orford, a widow, schoolmistress of the Borough
Captain Balstrode, a retired merchant skipper
Auntie, landlady of 'The Boar'
Niece 1, Niece 2, main attractions of 'The Boar'
Robert Boles, fisherman and Methodist
Swallow, a lawyer
Mrs (Nabob) Sedley, a rentier widow of an East India Company's
                   factor
Rev. Horace Adams, the rector
Ned Keene, apothecary and quack
Dr. Crabbe
Hobson, carrier
Chorus of townspeople and fisherfolk

**Scene:** The Borough, a small fishing town on the East Coast
**Time:** Towards 1830

## Prologue

*Interior of the Moot Hall, arranged as for Coroner's Inquest. Coroner, Mr Swallow, at table on daïs, clerk at table below. A crowd of townspeople in the body of the hall is kept back by Hobson acting as Constable. Mr Swallow is the leading lawyer of the Borough and at the same time its Mayor and its Coroner. A man of unexceptionable career and talents, he nevertheless disturbs the burgesses by his air of a man with an arrière-pensée.*

Hobson      *(shouts)* Peter Grimes

*(Peter Grimes steps forward from among the crowd.)*

Swallow     Peter Grimes, we are here to investigate the cause of
              death of your apprentice, William Spode, whose body

whose body you brought ashore from your boat, 'The Boy Billy', on the 26th ultimo. Do you wish to give evidence?

*(Peter nods.)*

Will you step into the box. Peter Grimes. Take the oath. After me. I swear by Almighty God.

| | |
|---|---|
| Peter | I swear by Almighty God. |
| Swallow | That the evidence I shall give. |
| Peter | That the evidence I shall give. |
| Swallow | Shall be the truth. |
| Peter | Shall be the truth. |
| Swallow | The whole truth and nothing but the truth. |
| Peter | The whole truth and nothing but the truth. |
| Swallow | Tell the court the story in your own words. |

*(Peter is silent.)*

You sailed your boat round the coast with the intention of putting in at London. Why did you do this?

| | |
|---|---|
| Peter | We had a huge catch, too big to sell here. |
| Swallow | And the boy died on the way? |
| Peter | The wind turned against us, blew us off our course. We ran out of drinking water. |
| Swallow | How long were you at sea? |
| Peter | Three days. |
| Swallow | What happened next? |
| Peter | He died lying there among the fish. |
| Swallow | What did you do? |
| Peter | Threw them all overboard and sailed for home. |
| Swallow | You mean you threw the fish overboard?... When you landed did you call for help? |
| Peter | I called Ned Keene. |
| Swallow | The apothecary here? *(indicates Ned)* Was there anybody else called? |
| Peter | Somebody brought the parson. |
| Swallow | You mean the Rector, Mr Horace Adams? |

*(The Rector steps forward. Swallow waves him back.)*

All right, Mr Adams.

*(He turns back to Peter.)*

|            |                                                                                |
| ---------- | ------------------------------------------------------------------------------ |
|            | Was there a certain amount of excitement?                                      |
| Peter      | Bob Boles started shouting.                                                    |
| Swallow    | There was a scene in the village street from which you were rescued by our landlady? |
| Peter      | Yes. By Auntie.                                                                |
| Swallow    | We don't call her that here...You then took to abusing a respectable lady.     |

*(Peter glares.)*

Answer me... You shouted abuse at a certain person?

*Mrs Sedley pushes forward. Mrs Sedley is the widow of a retired factor of the East India Company and is known locally as 'Mrs Nabob'. She is 65, self-assertive, inquisitive, unpopular.*

|            |                                          |
| ---------- | ---------------------------------------- |
| Mrs Sedley | Say who, say who.                        |
| Swallow    | Mrs Sedley here.                         |
| Peter      | *(fiercely)* I don't like interferers.   |

*A slight hubbub among the spectators resolves itself into a chorus which is more like the confused muttering of a crowd than something fully articulate.*

|                   |                                                                                               |
| ----------------- | --------------------------------------------------------------------------------------------- |
| Chorus            | When women gossip the result                                                                  |
|                   | Is someone doesn't sleep at night.                                                            |
| Hobson            | *(shouting)* Silence!                                                                          |
| Swallow           | Now tell me this. Who helped you carry the boy home? The schoolmistress, the widow, Mrs Ellen Orford? |
| Women's<br>Chorus | When a man prays he shuts his eyes                                                             |
|                   | And so can't tell the truth from lies.                                                         |
| Hobson            | *(shouts)* Silence.                                                                            |
| Swallow           | Mrs Orford, as the schoolmistress, the widow, how did you come into this?                     |
| Ellen             | I did what I could to help.                                                                    |
| Swallow           | Why should you help this kind of fellow – callous, brutal, and coarse? *(to Grimes)* There's something |

here perhaps in your favour. I'm told you rescued
this boy from drowning in the March storms.

*(Peter is silent.)*

Have you something else to say?
No? – Then I have.
Peter Grimes, I here advise you – do not get another
boy apprentice. Get a fisherman to help you – big
enough to stand up for himself. Our verdict is – that
William Spode, your apprentice, died in accidental
circumstances. But that's the kind of thing people are
apt to remember.

Chorus    But when the crowner sits upon it,
          Who can dare to fix the guilt?

Hobson    *(shouts)* Silence! Silence!

*(Peter has stepped forward and is trying to speak).*

Peter     Your honour! Like every other fisherman I have to
          hire an apprentice. I must have help –

Swallow   Then get a woman help you look after him.

Peter     That's what I want – but not yet –

Swallow   Why not?

Peter     Not till I've stopped people's mouths.

*(The hubbub begins again.)*

Swallow   *(makes a gesture of dismissal)*
          Stand down! Clear the court. Stand down!

Peter     Stand down you say. You wash your hands.
          The case goes on in people's minds
          And charges that no court has made
          Will be shouted at my head.
          Let me speak, let me stand trial,
          Bring the accusers into the hall.
          O let me thrust into their mouths,
          The truth itself, the simple truth.

*(He shouts this excitedly against the hubbub chorus.)*

Chorus    When women gossip, the result
          Is someone doesn't sleep at night.
          But when the crowner sits upon it,

Who can dare to fix the guilt?

*(Against them all Constable Hobson shouts his:)*

Hobson      Clear the court.

*Swallow rises with slow dignity. Everybody stands up while he makes his ceremonial exit. The crowd then begins to go out. Peter and Ellen are left alone.*

Peter       The truth – the pity – and the truth.
Ellen       Peter, come home.
Peter       Where the walls themselves
            Gossip of inquest!
Ellen       But we'll gossip, too,
            And eat and rest.
Peter       While Peeping Toms
            Nod as you go.
            You'll share the name
            Of outlaw, too.
Ellen       Peter, we shall restore your name.
            Warmed by the new esteem
            That you will find.
Peter       Until the Borough hate
            Poisons your mind.
Ellen       There'll be new shoals to catch:
            Life will be kind.
Peter       Ay! only of drowning ghosts:
            O, Time will not forget:
            The dead are witness
            And fate is Blind.
Both        Your voice out of the pain,
            Is like a hand
            That I can feel and know:
            Here is a friend.

*They walk off slowly as the CURTAIN FALLS.*

**Act One**
**Scene 1**

*Street by the sea: Moot Hall exterior with its outside staircase, next door to which is 'The Boar'. Ned Keene's apothecary's shop is at the street corner. On the other side breakwaters run down to the sea. It is morning, before high tide, several days later. Two fishermen are turning the capstan, hauling in their boat. Prolonged cries as the boat is hauled ashore. Women come from mending nets to take the fish baskets from other fishermen who now disembark.*

*Captain Balstrode sits on the breakwater looking out to sea through his glasses. Balstrode is a retired merchant sea-captain, shrewd as a travelled man should be, but with a general sympathy that makes him the favourite rentier of the whole Borough. He chews a plug of tobacco while he watches.*

*Chorus of Fishermen and Women*

| | |
|---|---|
| Chorus | Oh hang at open doors the net cork |
| | While squalid sea-dames at their mending work |
| | Welcome the hour when fishing through the tide |
| | The weary husband throws his freight aside. |
| Fishermen | O cold and wet and driven with the tide |
| | Beat your tired arms against your tarry side. |
| | Find rest in public bars where watery gin |
| | Will aid the warmth that languishes within. |

*(Several fishermen cross to 'The Boar where Auntie stands in the doorway.)*

| | |
|---|---|
| Fisherman | Auntie! |
| Auntie | Come in gentlemen, come in. |
| Boles | O her vats flow with poisoned gin. |

*(Boles the Methodist fisherman stands aside from all this dram drinking.)*

| | |
|---|---|
| Fisherman | Boles has gone Methody. *(points and laughs.)* |
| Auntie | A man should have |
| | Hobbies to cheer his private life. |

*(Fishermen go into 'The Boar'. Others remain with their wives at the nets and boats.)*

Chorus          Dabbling on shore half-naked sea-boys crowd
                Swim round a ship, or swing upon a shroud:
                Or in a boat purloined with paddles play
                And grow familiar with the watery way.

*(While the second boat is being hauled in, boys are scrambling over the first.)*

Balstrode       Shoo, you little barnacles
                Up your anchors, hoist your sails.

*Balstrode chases them from the boat. A more respectable figure now begins, with much hat-raising, his morning progress down the High Street. He makes straight for 'The Boar'.*

1st Fisher      *(touches cap).*  Dr. Crabbe.
Boles           *(points as the swing door closes.)*
                He drinks 'Good Health' to all diseases.
Fisherwoman     Storm?
2nd Fisher      Storm?

*(They shade their eyes looking out to sea.)*

Balstrode       *(glass to his eye)*
                A long way out. Sea horses.
                The wind is holding back the tide.
                If it veers round, watch for your lives.


Chorus of       And if the spring tide eats the land again
Fishers         Till even the cottages and cobbled walks of fishermen
                Are billets for the thievish waves which take
                As if in sleep, thieving for thieving's sake –

*The Rector comes down the High Street. He is followed as always by the Borough's second most famous rentier, the widow, Mrs (Nabob) Sedley. From The Boar come the two 'nieces' who give Auntie her nickname. They stand in front of the pub taking the morning sun. Ned Keene, seeing Mrs Sedley, pops out of his shop door.*

Rector          *(right and left).* Good morning, good morning!
Nieces          Good morning!

| Mrs Sedley | Good morning. Good morning, dear Rector. |
| Ned | Had Auntie no nieces we'd never respect her. |
| Swallow | Good morning! Good morning! |
| Nieces | Good morning! |
| Mrs Sedley | Good morning, your worship, Mr Swallow. |
| Auntie | *(to Keene)* |
| | You jeer, but if they wink you're eager to follow! |

*(The Rector and Mrs Sedley continue towards the Church.)*

| Ned | *(shouts across to Auntie).* |
| | I'm coming tonight to see your nieces. |
| Auntie | *(dignified).* 'The Boar' is at its patron's service. |
| Boles | God's storm will drown your hot desires! |
| Balstrode | God stay the tide, or I shall share your fears. |
| Chorus | For us sea-dwellers, this sea-birth can be |
| | Death to our gardens of fertility. |
| | Yet only such contemptuous springtide can |
| | Tickle the virile impotence of man. |
| Peter | *(calls off).* Hi! Give us a hand! |

(Chorus stops).

| Peter | Haul the boat! |
| Boles | (shouts back). Haul it yourself, Grimes! |
| Peter | *(off).* Somebody bring the rope! |

*Nobody does. Presently he appears and takes the capstan rope himself and pulls it after him (off) to the boat. Then he returns. The fishermen and women turn their backs on him and slouch away awkwardly.*

| Balstrode | *(at capstan).* I'll give a hand, the tide is near the turn. |
| Keene | *(at capstan).* We'll drown the gossips in a tidal storm. |
| Auntie | *(at the door of 'The Boar')* |
| | Parsons may moralise and fools decide, |
| | But a good publican takes neither side |
| | And if a man drinks quiet and can pay |
| | No decent landlady turns trade away. |
| Balstrode | *(turning capstan).* |
| | O haul away! The tide is near the turn. |
| Keene | *(turning capstan).* |

|  |  |
|---|---|
|  | Man invented morals but tides have none. |
| Boles | *(with arms akimbo watches their labour)* |
|  | This lost soul of a fisherman must be |
|  | Shunned by respectable society. |
|  | Oh let the captains hear, the scholars learn: |
|  | Shielding the sin they share the people's scorn. |
| Auntie | I have my business. Let the preachers learn |
|  | Hell may be fiery but the pub won't burn. |
| Balstrode and Keene | |
|  | The tide that floods will ebb |
|  | The tide, the tide will turn. |

*(The boat is hauled up. Grimes appears.)*

| Ned | Grimes, you won't need help from now. I've got a prentice for you. |
|---|---|
| Balstrode | A workhouse brat? |
| Keene | I called at the workhouse yesterday. |
|  | All you do now is fetch the boy. |
|  | We'll send the Carrier with a note. |
|  | He'll bring your bargain on his cart. |
|  | (shouts) Jim Hobson, we've a job for you. |
| Hobson | (enters). Cart's full sir. More than I can do. |
| Keene | Listen, Jim. You'll go to the workhouse |
|  | And ask for Mr Ned Keene's purchase. |
|  | Bring him back to Grimes. |
| Hobson | Cart's full, sir. I have no room. |
| Ned | Hobson, you'll do what there is to be done. |

*(It is near enough to an argument to attract a crowd. Fishermen and women gather round. Boles takes his chance.)*

| Boles | Is this a Christian country? Are |
|---|---|
|  | Workhouse children so enslaved |
|  | That their bodies sell for cash? |
| Ned | Hobson. Will you do your job? |

*Ellen Orford has come in. She is a widow of about 40. Her children have died, or grown up and gone away, and in her loneliness she has become the Borough schoolmistress. A hard life has not hardened her. It has made her the more charitable.*

| | |
|---|---|
| Hobson | I have to go from pub to pub |
| | Picking up parcels, standing about |
| | My journey back is late at night. |
| | Mister, find some other road |
| | To bring your boy back. |
| Chorus | He's right. |
| Hobson | Mister, find some other road... |
| Ellen | Carter! I'll mind your passenger. |
| Chorus | What? And be Grimes's messenger? |
| Ellen | Whatever you say, I'm not ashamed. |
| | Somebody must do the job. |
| | The carter goes from pub to pub, |
| | Picking up parcels, standing about. |
| | The boy needs comfort late at night. |
| | He needs a welcome on the road. |
| | Coming here strange he'll be afraid. |
| | I'll mind your passenger! |
| Ned | Mrs Orford is talking sense. |
| Chorus | Ellen – you're leading us a dance, |
| | Fetching boys for Peter Grimes, |
| | Because the Borough is afraid |
| | You who help will share the blame. |
| Ellen | Let her among you without fault |
| | Cast the first stone |
| | And let the Pharisees and Sadducees |
| | Give way to none. |
| | But whosoever feels his pride |
| | Humbled so deep |
| | There is no corner he can hide |
| | Even in sleep |
| | Will have no trouble to find out |
| | How a poor teacher |
| | Widowed and lonely finds delight |
| | In shouldering care. |
| Ellen | *(as she moves up the street)* |

Mr. Hobson, where's your cart?

| | |
|---|---|
| Hobson | Up here, ma'am. I can wait. |

*(The crowd stands round and watches. Some follow Ellen and*

*Hobson. On the edge of the crowd are other activities.)*

| | |
|---|---|
| Mrs Sedley | *(whispers to Ned).*  Have you my pills? |
| Ned | I'm sorry, mum. |
| Mrs Sedley | My sleeping draught. |
| Ned | The laudanum |
| | Is out of stock, and being brought |
| | By Mr Carrier Hobson's cart. |
| | He's back tonight. |
| Mrs Sedley | Good Lord, good Lord – |
| Ned | Meet us both at this pub, 'The Boar' |
| | Auntie's we call it. It's quite safe. |
| Mrs Sedley | I've never been in a pub in my life. |
| Ned | You'll come? |
| Mrs Sedley | All right. |
| Ned | Tonight? |
| Mrs Sedley | All right. |

*(She moves off up the street.)*

| | |
|---|---|
| Ned | If the old dear takes much more laudanum |
| | She'll land herself one day in Bedlam! |
| Balstrode | (looks seaward through his glass) |
| | Look! The storm come! |
| | The wind veers |
| | In from the sea |
| | At gale force. |
| Chorus | Shutter your windows! |
| | And bring in all the nets! |
| | |
| | Now the flood tide |
| | And the sea-horses |
| | Will gallop over |
| | The eroded coast |
| | |
| | Flooding, flooding |
| | Our seasonal fears. |
| | Look! The storm come |
| | The wind veers. |
| | |
| | A high tide coming |
| | Will eat the land |

A tide no breakwaters withstand.
Fasten your boats. The springtide's here
With a gale behind.

Is there much to fear?

| | |
|---|---|
| Ned | Only for the goods you're rich in: |
| | It won't drown your conscience; it might flood your |
| | kitchen. |
| Boles | *(passionately)* |
| | God has his ways which are not ours: |
| | His high tide swallows up the shores. |
| | Repent! |
| Ned | And keep your wife upstairs. |
| Omnes | O Tide that waits for no man |
| | Spare our coasts! |

*There is a general exeunt – mostly through the swing doors of 'The Boar'. Dr. Crabbe's hat blows away, is rescued for him by Ned Keene, who bows him into the pub. Finally only Peter and Balstrode are left, Peter gazing seaward, Balstrode hesitating at the pub door.*

| | |
|---|---|
| Balstrode | And do you prefer the storm |
| | To Auntie's parlour and the rum? |
| Peter | I live alone. The habit grows. |
| Balstrode | Grimes, since you're a lonely soul |
| | Born to blocks and spars and ropes |
| | Why not try the wider sea |
| | With merchantman or privateer? |
| Peter | I am native, rooted here. |
| Balstrode | Rooted by what? |
| Peter | By familiar fields, |
| | Mudbanks, sand, |
| | Ordinary streets, |
| | The prevailing wind. |
| Balstrode | You'd slip these moorings if you had the mind. |
| Peter | By the shut faces |
| | Of the Borough clans; |
| | By the forgiveness |
| | Of a casual glance. |
| Balstrode | You'll find no comfort there. |

|           | When an urchin's quarrelsome |
|           | Brawling at his childish games, |
|           | Mother stops him with the threat, |
|           | 'You'll be sold to Peter Grimes!' |
| Peter     | They sell me new apprentices, |
|           | Children taught to be ashamed |
|           | Of the legend on their faces – |
|           | 'You've been sold to Peter Grimes!'. |
| Balstrode | Then the coroner sits to |
|           | Hint, but not to mention crimes, |
|           | And publishes an open verdict |
|           | Whispered about this Peter Grimes. |
|           | Your boy was workhouse starved – |
|           | Maybe you're not to blame he died. |
| Peter     | Picture what my life was like |
|           | Tied to a child – |

Whose loneliness, despair
Flooded the cabin:
I launched the boat to find
Comfort in fishing.

Then the sea rose to a storm
Over the gunwales,
And the child's silent reproach
Turned to illness.

And I watched
Among fishing nets,
Alone, alone, alone
With a childish death!

| Balstrode | This storm is useful. You can speak your mind |
|           | And never fear the Borough commentary. |
|           | There is a grandeur in a gale of wind |
|           | To free confession, set a conscience free. |
| Peter     | They listen to money |
|           | These Borough gossips |
|           | I'll fish the sea dry |
|           | Swamp their markets, |
|           | Get money to choke |

|           | Down rumour's throat. |
|           | When others shelter |
|           | In the bad weather |
|           | I'll slip the painter. |
| Balstrode | With your new prentice? |
| Peter     | We'll sail together. |
|           | The Borough gossips |
|           | Listen to rumour |
|           | Listen to money: |
|           | One buys the other. |
|           | I shall buy rumour – |
|           | The wealthy merchant |
|           | Grimes will set up |
|           | House, home and shop |
|           | You will all see it! |
|           | I'll marry Ellen! |
| Balstrode | Man – go and ask her |
|           | Without your booty, |
|           | She'll have you now. |
| Peter     | No – not for pity!... |
| Balstrode | Then the old tragedy |
|           | Is in store: |
|           | New start with new prentice |
|           | Just as before. |
| Peter     | I prayed for luck always. |
|           | I pray once more. |
| Balstrode | You fool, man, fool! |

*(The wind has risen. Balstrode is shouting above it. Peter faces him angrily.)*

| Peter     | Are you my conscience? |
| Balstrode | Might as well |
|           | Try shout the wind down as to tell |
|           | The obvious truth. |
| Peter     | Take your advice – |
|           | Put it where your money is. |
| Balstrode | The storm is here. O come away. |
| Peter     | The storm is here and I shall stay. |

The storm is rising. Auntie comes out of 'The Boar' to fasten the shutters, in front of the windows. Balstrode goes to help her. He looks back towards Peter, then goes into the pub.

Peter *(alone)*   What harbour shelters peace?
                Away from tidal waves, away from storm
                What harbour can embrace
                Terrors and tragedies?
                With her there'll be no quarrels,
                This time the mood will stay,
                Her breast is harbour too –
                But they... but they... but they....

*(The wind rises. He stands a moment as if leaning against the wind.)*

CURTAIN

## Act I
## Scene 2

*Interior of 'The Boar', typical main room of a country pub. No bar. Upright settles, tables, log fire. When the curtain rises Auntie is admitting Mrs Sedley. The gale has risen to hurricane force and Auntie holds the door with difficulty against the wind which rattles the windows and howls in the chimney. They both push the door closed.*

| | |
|---|---|
| Auntie | Past time to close. |
| Mrs Sedley | He said half-past ten. |
| Auntie | Who? |
| Mrs Sedley | Mr Keene. |
| Auntie | Him and his women! |
| Mrs Sedley | You referring to me? |
| Auntie | Not at all, not at all. |
| | What do you want? |
| Mrs Sedley | Room from the storm. |
| Auntie | This is the sort of weak politeness |
| | Makes a publican lose her clients. |
| | Keep in the corner out of sight. |

*(Balstrode and a Fisherman enter. They struggle with the door.)*

| | |
|---|---|
| Balstrode | Phew, that's a bitch of a gale all right. |
| Auntie | *(nods her head towards Mrs Sedley).* Sh-h-h. |
| Balstrode | Sorry. I didn't see you, missis. |
| | You'll give the regulars a surprise, |
| Auntie | She's meeting Ned. |
| Balstrode | Which Ned? |
| Auntie | The quack. |
| | He's looking after her heart attack. |
| Balstrode | Bring us a pint. |
| Auntie | It's closing time. |
| Balstrode | You fearful old female – why should you mind? |
| Auntie | The storm. |

*(Bob Boles and other fishermen enter. The wind howls through the door and again there is difficulty in closing it.)*

| Boles | Did you hear the tide |
|---|---|
| | Has broken over the Northern Road? |

*He leaves the door open too long with disastrous consequences. A sudden gust howls through the door, the shutters of the window fly open, a pane blows in)*

| Balstrode | *(shouts)* Get those shutters. |
|---|---|
| Auntie | *(screams)* O-o-o-o-o! |
| Balstrode | You fearful old female, why do you |
| | Leave your windows naked? |
| Auntie | O-o-o-o-o! |
| Balstrode | Better strip a niece or two |
| | And clamp your shutters! |

*The two 'nieces' run in. They are young, pretty enough though a little worn, conscious that they are the chief attraction of 'The Boar.' At the moment they are in mild hysterics, having run downstairs in their night clothes, though with their unusual instinct for precaution they have found time to don each a wrap. It is not clear whether they are sisters, friends or simply colleagues: but they behave like twins, as though each has only half a personality and they cling together always to sustain their self-esteem.*

| Nieces | Oo! Oo! Oo! |
|---|---|
| | It's blown our bedroom windows in. |
| | Oo! we'll all be drowned. |
| Balstrode | Perhaps in gin. |
| Nieces | I wouldn't mind if it didn't howl. |
| | It gets on my nerves. |
| | We'll all be drowned. |
| | wouldn't mind if it didn't howl. |
| Balstrode | D'you think we |
| | Should stop our storm for such as you – |
| | Coming all over palpitations! |
| | Auntie, get some new relations. |
| Auntie | (takes it ill) Loud man, I never did have time |
| | For the sort of creature who spits in his wine. |
| | A joke's a joke and fun is fun, |
| | But say your grace and be polite for all that we have done. |

| Nieces | For your peace of mind. |
|---|---|
| Mrs Sedley | This is no place for me! |
| Auntie | Loud man, you're glad enough to be |
| | Playing your cards in our company. |
| | A joke's a joke and fun is fun, |
| | But say your grace and be polite for all that we have |
| | done. |
| Nieces | For your peace of mind. |
| Mrs Sedley | This is no place for me! |
| Auntie | Loud man— |

*(Two Fishermen enter. Usual struggle with the door.)*

| 1st Fisher | There's been a landslide up the coast. |
|---|---|
| Boles | (rising unsteadily). I'm drunk. Drunk. |
| Balstrode | You're a Methody wastrel. |
| Boles | (staggers to one of the nieces). Is this a niece of yours? |
| Auntie | That's so. |
| Boles | Who's her father? |
| Auntie | Who wants to know? |
| Boles | I want to pay my best respects |
| | To the beauty and misery of her sex. |
| Balstrode | Old Methody, you'd better tune |
| | Your piety to another hymn. |
| Boles | I want her. |
| Balstrode | Sh-h-h. |
| Auntie | *(cold)* Turn that man out. |
| Balstrode | Auntie, he's the local preacher. |
| | He's lost the way of carrying liquor. |
| | He means no harm. |
| Boles | No, I mean love. |

*(Boles hits him. Mrs Sedley screams. Balstrode quietly overpowers Boles and sits him in a chair.)*

| Balstrode | We live and let live – and look – |
|---|---|
| | We keep our hands to ourselves. |

*(Boles struggles to his feet. Balstrode sits him down again, laying the law down.)*

| Balstrode | Pub conversation should depend |
|---|---|

On this eternal moral;
The satire never should descend
To fisticuff or quarrel,
We live and let live, and look
We keep our hands to ourselves.

*(And while Boles is being forced into his chair again, the bystanders comment:)*

| | |
|---|---|
| Chorus | We live and let live, and look |
| | We keep our hands to ourselves. |
| Balstrode | We sit and drink the evening through |
| | Not deigning to devote a |
| | Thought to the daily cud we chew |
| | But buying drinks by rota. |
| | We live and let live, and look |
| | We keep our hands to ourselves. |

*And chorus as before*

*Door opens. The struggle with the wind is worse than before as Ned Keene gets through.*

| | |
|---|---|
| Ned | Have you heard the cliff is down |
| | Up by Peter Grimes's hut? |
| Mrs Sedley | Thank God you've come! |
| Ned | You won't blow away. |
| Mrs Sedley | That Carter's over half an hour late. |
| Balstrode | He'll be later still: the road's under flood. |
| Mrs Sedley | I can't stay longer. I refuse. |
| Ned | You'll have to stay if you want your pills. |
| Mrs Sedley | With drunken females and in brawls! |
| Ned | They're Auntie's nieces, that's what they are |
| | And better than you for kissing, ma. |
| | Mind that door! |
| All | Mind that door! |

*(The door opens again. Peter Grimes has come in. Unlike the rest he wears no oilskins. His hair looks wild.)*

| | |
|---|---|
| Chorus | Talk of the devil and there he is |
| | A devil he is, and a devil he is. |
| | Grimes is waiting his apprentice. |

*Grimes advances into the room, shaking off the raindrops from his hair. Mrs Sedley faints. Ned Keene catches her as she falls.)*

| Ned | Get the brandy, aunt. |
| Auntie | Who'll pay? |
| Ned | Her. I'll charge her for it. |

*(Peter sits down. The others move away from that side of the table.)*

| Ned | This widow's as strong as any eight |
| | Fisherwomen I have met. |
| | Everybody's very quiet. |

*(No-one answers. Silence is broken by Peter, but his words are not addressed to the company.)*

| Peter | Now the great Bear and Pleiades |
| | where earth moves |
| | Are drawing up the clouds |
| | of human grief |
| | Breathing solemnity in the deep night. |
| | Who can decipher |
| | in storm or starlight |
| | The written character |
| | of a friendly fate— |
| | As the sky turns, the world for us to change? |
| | But if the horoscope's |
| | bewildering |
| | Like a flashing turmoil |
| | of a shoal of herring, |
| | Who can turn skies back and begin again? |

*(Silence again. Then muttering in undertones.)*

| Chorus | He's mad or drunk. |
| | Why's that man here? |
| Nieces | His song alone would sour the beer. |
| Chorus | The devil spoke. |
| | O chuck him out. |
| Nieces | I wouldn't mind if he didn't howl. |
| Chorus | He looks as though he's nearly drowned. |
| Boles | *(staggers up to Grimes).* |
| | You've sold your soul, Grimes. |

| | |
|---|---|
| Balstrode | Come away. |
| Boles | Satan's has no hold on me. |
| Balstrode | Leave him alone, you drunkard there. |

*(Goes to get hold of Boles.)*

| | |
|---|---|
| Boles | I'll hold the gospel light before<br>The cataract that blinds his eyes. |

*(Grimes thrusts Boles aside roughly and turns away.)*

| | |
|---|---|
| Boles | His exercise<br>Is not with men but killing boys. |

*Boles picks up a bottle and is about to bring it down on Grimes's head when Balstrode knocks it out of his hand and it crashes in fragments on the floor.*

| | |
|---|---|
| Auntie | For God's sake, help me keep the peace.<br>D'you want me up at the next Assize? |
| Balstrode | For peace sake, someone start a song. |

*(Keene starts a round.)*

| | |
|---|---|
| Auntie | That's right, Ned! |
| All | Old Joe has gone fishing and<br>Young Joe has gone fishing and<br>You Know has gone fishing and<br>Found them a shoal.<br>Pull them in handfuls,<br>And in canfuls,<br>And in panfuls<br>Bring them in sweetly,<br>Gut them completely,<br>Pack them up neatly,<br>Sell them discretely,<br>Oh, haul a-way. |

*(Peter comes into the round: the others stop.)*

| | |
|---|---|
| Peter | When I had gone fishing<br>When he had gone fishing<br>When You Know'd gone fishing<br>We found him Davy Jones.<br>Bring him in with horror, |

         Bring him with terror,
         And bring him in with sorrow!
         Oh, haul a-way.

*This breaks the round, but the others recover in a repeat.*

*At the climax of the round the door opens to admit Ellen Orford, the boy and the carrier. All three are soaking, muddy and bedraggled.*

Hobson     The bridge is down, we half swam over.
Ned        And your cart? Is it seaworthy?

*(The women go to Ellen and the boy. Auntie fusses over them. Boles reproaches.)*

Boles      *(to Ellen)* Serves you right, woman.
Auntie     My dear
           There's brandy and hot water to spare.
Nieces     Let's look at the boy.
Ellen      *(rising).* Let him be.
Nieces     *(admiring).* Nice sweet thing.
Ellen      *(protecting him).* Not for such as you.
Peter      Let's go. You ready?
Auntie     Let them warm up
           They've been half drowned.
Peter      Time to get off.
Auntie     Your hut's washed away.
Peter      Only the cliff.
           Young prentice come.
           Young prentice home.

*(He takes the boy out into the storm.)*

CURTAIN

## Act II
## Scene 1

*Scene as in Act One. The Street. A fine, sunny morning, some weeks later. The street is deserted till Ellen and the boy, John, enter. Ellen is carrying a workbasket. She sits down between a boat and a breakwater and takes her knitting from the basket. One or two late-comers cross and hurry into the church.*

Ellen  The sun in
     His own morning
     And upward climb
     Makes the world warm.

     Night rolled
     Away with cold.
     The summer morning
I      s for growing.

*(The organ starts voluntary in church.)*

     Shall we not go to church this Sunday
     And do our knitting by the sea?

*(Hymn [off].)*

     Now that the daylight fills the sky
     We lift our hearts to God on high
     That He in all we do or say
     Would keep us free from harm to-day.
Ellen  I'll do the work. You talk.
     Nothing to tell me? Then shall I
     Guess what your life was like and you
     See if I'm right?
     I believe
     You liked your workhouse with its grave,
     Empty look. You liked to be
     A lonely fellow in your misery.
     When I became a teacher
     I thought of school as bleak and bare –
     Then found it the sort of place
     I daresay like your own workhouse

> Where the woes of little people
> Hurt more, but are more simple.

*(She goes on with her work. John says nothing.)*

Congregation *(in church)*
> May He restrain our tongues from strife
> And shield from anger's din our life
> And guard with watchful care our eyes
> From earth's absorbing vanities.

Ellen
> John, you know what an inquest is.
> You may have heard some of the stories
> Of the prentice Peter had before.

*(Hymn continues, third verse.)*

> And when you came, I
> Said, Now this is where we
> Take things in hand. Does this
> Sound like interferences?

*(Morning prayer begins. The Rector's voice is heard.)*

Rector
> Wherefore I pray and beseech you, as many as are
> here present, to accompany me with a pure heart
> and humble voice, saying after me...

Congregation
> Almighty and most merciful Father, we have
> erred and strayed from Thy ways like lost sheep.

*(The prayer continues through the ensuing scene.)*

Ellen
> There's a tear in your coat. Was that done
> Before you came?... Badly torn.
> That was done recently.
> Take your hand away.
> Your neck is it? John,
> What are you trying to hide?

Choir *(in church)*
> O Lord, open Thou our lips;
> And our mouth shall shew forth Thy praise.
> O God make speed to save us
> O Lord make haste to help us.

*(Ellen undoes the neck of shirt.)*

| | |
|---|---|
| Ellen | A bruise. Well...it's begun. |
| Choir | Glory be to the Father and to the Son and to the Holy Ghost. As it was in the beginning is now and ever shall be world without end. Amen. |
| Ellen | Child, you're not too young to know |
| | Where roots of sorrow are |
| | Innocent you've learned how near |
| | Life is to torture. |
| | Death's tremendous wings are less |
| | Frightening than shapelessness. |
| | Life childishly needs holidays |
| | Like God needs praise. |
| | Let this day then be to us |
| | Sun and sea and quietness |
| | While the treason of the waves |
| | Glitters like love's. |
| Choir *(off)* | O all ye works of the Lord, bless ye the Lord |
| | O ye Sun and Moon, bless ye the Lord |
| | O ye stars of Heaven, bless ye the Lord |
| | O ye Winds of God, bless ye the Lord, |
| | Praise Him and magnify Him for ever. |

*(Peter Grimes enters.)*

| | |
|---|---|
| Choir *(off)* | O ye Light and Darkness, bless ye the Lord |
| | O ye Nights and Days, bless ye the Lord |
| | O ye Lightnings and Clouds, bless ye the Lord, |
| | Praise Him and magnify Him for ever. |
| Peter | Come boy. |
| Ellen | Peter – what for? |
| Choir *(off)* | O ye wells, bless ye the Lord |
| | O ye seas and floods, bless the Lord, |
| | O ye whales and all that move in the waters |
| | Praise Him and magnify Him for ever. |
| Peter | I need his help. I've seen a shoal. |
| Ellen | But if there were then all the boats |
| | Would fast be launching. |
| Peter | I can find |
| | The shoals to which the rest are blind. |
| Choir *(off)* | O all ye fowls of the air, bless ye the Lord |

|        |                                                    |
|--------|----------------------------------------------------|
|        | O all ye beasts and cattle, bless ye the Lord      |
|        | O ye children of Men, bless ye the Lord            |
|        | Praise Him and magnify Him forever.                |
| Ellen  | This is a Sunday, his day of rest.                 |
| Peter  | This is whatever day I say it is!                  |
|        | Come boy!                                          |
| Ellen  | You and John have fished all week                  |
|        | Night and day at endless work                      |
|        | Painting boat and mending nets,                    |
|        | Now let him rest.                                  |
| Peter  | Come boy! Come boy!                                 |
| Ellen  | But your bargain...                                 |
| Peter  | What boy I have body and soul he's mine.           |
| Ellen  | Hush, Peter, Hush!                                 |
| Choir *(off)* | O ye servants of the Lord, bless ye the Lord |
|        | O ye holy and humble, bless ye the Lord            |
|        | Ananias, Azarias and Misael, bless ye the Lord     |
|        | Praise Him and magnify Him forever.                |
|        | As it was in the beginning is now and ever shall be, |
|        | world without end. Amen.                           |

*(The sounds dies down. In church the lesson is being read.)*

|        |                                                    |
|--------|----------------------------------------------------|
| Ellen  | Peter, this unforgiving work                       |
|        | This grey, unresting industry,                     |
|        | What aim, what future does it mark                 |
|        | What peace will your hard profits buy?             |
| Peter  | Buy us a home, buy us esteem                        |
|        | And buy us freedom from pain                       |
|        | Of grinning at gossip's tale                       |
|        | Believe, believe, we'll buy our fate.              |
| Choir  | *(in church)*                                      |
|        | I Believe in God the Father, God the Son and God   |
|        | the Holy Ghost, and in Jesus Christ his only Son... |

*(Fades into background.)*

|        |                                                    |
|--------|----------------------------------------------------|
| Ellen  | Peter, tell me one thing, where                    |
|        | The youngster got that ugly bruise?                |
| Peter  | Out of the hurly burly!                            |
| Ellen  | O your ways                                        |

|          |                                      |
|----------|--------------------------------------|
|          | Are hard and rough beyond his days.  |
|          | Peter, were we right in what we planned |
|          | To do? Were we right, were we right? |
| Peter    | Take away your hand.                 |
|          | *(then quietly)*                     |
|          | My only hope depends on you.         |
|          | If you – take it away – what's left? |
| Ellen    | Were we mistaken when we schemed     |
|          | To solve your life by lonely toil?   |
|          | Were we mistaken when we dreamed     |
|          | That we'd come through and all be well? |
|          | Peter you cannot buy your peace      |
|          | You'll never stop the gossips' tale  |
|          | With all the fish from all the seas. |
| Peter.   | We should give in. We've failed.     |

*(He cries out as if in agony. Then strikes her. The basket falls.)*

| Peter | So be it! And God have mercy upon me! |
|-------|----------------------------------------|

*The boy runs from him. Peter follows. Ellen watches. Then goes out the other way. Behind closed doors and half-open windows neighbours have been watching. Three now emerge. First Auntie, then Ned Keene, finally Boles.*

| Auntie | Fool to let it come to this!         |
|--------|--------------------------------------|
|        | Wasting pity, squandering tears.     |
| Ned    | See the glitter in his eyes!         |
|        | Grimes is at his exercise.           |
| Boles  | What he fears is that the Lord       |
|        | Follows with a flaming sword.        |
| Auntie | You see all through crazy eyes.      |
| Ned    | Grimes is at his exercise.           |
| Boles  | Where's the pastor of this flock?    |
|        | Where's the guardian shepherd's hook? |
| All    | Parson, lawyer, clerks at prayers.   |

*(In the church the Benediction. The congregation emerges.)*

| Ned, Boles | Now the church parade begins,      |
|------------|------------------------------------|
| and Auntie | Fresh beginning for fresh sins.    |
|            | Ogling with a pious gaze           |

Each one's at his exercise.

*(Doctor Crabbe comes first.)*

| | |
|---|---|
| Auntie | Doctor! |
| Ned | Leave him out of this. |
| Mrs Sedley | *(from church)* What is it? |
| Ned | Private business. |
| Mrs Sedley | I heard two voices during psalms |
| | One was Grimes, and one more calm. |
| Boles | *(to a fisherwoman as she comes out)* |
| | *While you worshipped idols there* |
| | The Devil had his Sabbath here. |
| Balstrode | Grimes is weatherwise and skilled |
| | In the practice of his trade. |
| | Let him be, let us forget |
| | What slander can invent. |
| Chorus | What is it? |
| Auntie, | Boles and Ned |
| | What do you suppose? |
| | Grimes is at his exercise. |

*As people come out two by two, they circulate the village green singing their couplets as they reach the centre. First come Swallow and a fellow lawyer.*

| | |
|---|---|
| Chorus | What is it? What do you suppose? |
| | Grimes is at his exercise. |
| Fellow | Dullards build their self-esteem |
| Lawyer | By inventing cruelties. |
| Swallow | Even so, the law restrains |
| | Too impetuous enterprise. |
| Fisherwomen | *(chorus)* |
| | Fishing is a lonely trade |
| | Single men have much to bear. |
| Two Nieces | If a man's work can't be made |
| | Decent, let him stay ashore. |
| Chorus | *(over all)* |
| | What is it? What do you suppose? |
| | Grimes is at his exercise. |

*(Balstrode pauses by Ned as he walks round.)*

| | |
|---|---|
| Rector | My flock – oh what a weight is this |
| | Pastoral authority. |
| Mrs Sedley | And what a dangerous faith is this |
| | That gives souls equality! |
| Balstrode | When the Borough gossip starts |
| | Somebody must suffer for it. |
| Ned | And thanks to flinty human hearts |
| | Even quacks can make a profit. |
| Chorus | What is it? What do you suppose? |
| | Grimes is at his exercise. |

*(During the hubbub Boles climbs a little way up the steps of the Moot Hall.)*

| | |
|---|---|
| Boles | People... No. I will speak... |
| | This thing here concerns you all. |
| Chorus | *(crowding round Boles)* |
| | Whoever's guilty gets the rap |
| | The Borough keeps its standards up. |
| Balstrode | Tub-thumping. |
| Boles | O this prentice system |
| | Is uncivilized, unchristian. |
| Balstrode | Something of the sort befits |
| | Brats conceived outside the sheets. |
| Boles | Where's the parson in his black? |
| | Is he there or is he not? |
| | To guide a sinful straying flock? |
| Chorus | Where's the parson? |
| Rector | Is it my business? |
| Boles | Your business to ignore |
| | Growing at your door |
| | Evils, like your fancy flowers? |
| Chorus | Evils! |
| Rector | Calm now! Tell me what it is. |

*(Ellen comes in. She is met by Auntie who has picked up Ellen's abandoned basket and its contents.)*

| | |
|---|---|
| Auntie | Ellen dear, see I have gathered |
| | All your things. Come rest inside. |

| | |
|---|---|
| Boles and Chorus | She can tell you, Ellen Orford. |
| | She helped him in his cruel games. |
| Rector | *(holding his hand up for silence)* |
| | Ellen please. |
| Ellen | What am I to do? |
| Boles and Chorus | Speak out in the name of the Lord. |
| Ellen | We planned that their lives should |
| | Have a new start, |
| | That I, as a friend could |
| | Make the plan work |
| | By bringing comfort where |
| | Their lives were stark. |
| Rector | You planned to be worldly-wise |
| | But your souls were dark. |
| Ellen | We planned this time to |
| | Care for the boy; |
| | To save him from hardship |
| | Too hard to bear |
| | Mending his clothes and giving his |
| | Meals regular. |
| Swallow | You planned to heal sick souls |
| | With bodily care. |
| Mrs Sedley | O little care you for the prentice |
| | Or his welfare! |
| Boles | Call it danger, call it hardship |
| | Or plain murder! |
| Nieces | Perhaps his clothes you mended |
| | But you work his bones bare! |
| Auntie | You meant just to be kind |
| | And avert fear! |
| Balstrode | You interfering gossips, this |
| | Is not your business! |
| Hobson | Pity the boy! |
| Ellen | O pity those who try to bring |
| | A shadowed life into the sun. |
| Ellen, Auntie and Balstrode | O Lord, hard hearts! |

| Chorus | Who lets us down must take the rap |
| | The Borough keeps its standards up. |
| Omnes | *(without Ellen and Balstrode)* |
| | Tried to be kind! |
| | Murder! |
| | Tried to be kind and to help! |
| | Murder! |
| Rector | Swallow – shall we go and see Grimes in his home? |
| Swallow | Popular feeling's rising. |
| Rector | Balstrode. I'd like you to come. |
| Balstrode | I warn you. We shall waste our time. |
| Rector | I'd like your presence just the same. |
| Mrs Sedley | Little do the suspects know, |
| | I've the evidence. I have a clue. |
| Chorus | Now we shall find out the worst. |
| Rector | Only the men, the women stay. |
| Swallow | *(points to the nieces who join the crowd)* |
| | No ragtail no bobtail if you please. |
| Boles | *(pushes them away)* |
| | Back to the gutter – you keep out of this. |
| Rector | Mr Swallow. Come along. |
| Swallow | Carter Hobson, fetch the drum. |
| | Summon the Borough to Grimes's hut. |
| Chorus | To Grimes's hut! |
| | To Grimes's hut! |

*(He leads the way. Mrs Sedley and Swallow come next. Balstrode lags behind. Behind them come the rest of the crowd.)*

| Chorus | Now is gossip put on trial, |
| | Now the rumours either fail |
| | Or are shouted in the wind |
| | Sweeping furious through the land. |
| | |
| | Now the liars shiver for |
| | Now if they've cheated we shall know: |
| | We shall strike and strike to kill |
| | At the slander or the sin. |
| | |
| | Now the whisperer stands out |
| | Now confronted by the fact. |

> Bring the branding iron and knife:
> What's done now is done for life.

*(The crowd has gone. Auntie, Nieces and Ellen remain.)*

| | |
|---|---|
| Nieces | From the gutter, why should we |
| | Trouble at their ribaldries? |
| Auntie | And shall we be ashamed because |
| | We comfort men from ugliness? |
| All | Shall we smile or shall we weep |
| | Or wait quietly till they sleep? |
| Auntie | When in storm they shelter here |
| | And we soothe their fears away. |
| Nieces | We know they'll whistle their good-byes |
| | Next fine day and put to sea. |
| All | Shall we smile or shall we weep |
| | Or wait quietly till they sleep? |
| Ellen | Men are children when they strive |
| | We are mothers when they weep |
| | Schooling our own hearts to keep |
| | The bitter treasure of their love. |

CURTAIN

## Act II
## Scene 2

*Grimes's hut is an upturned boat. It is on the whole shipshape, though bare and forbidding. Ropes coiled, nets, kegs and casks furnish the place. It is lighted by a skylight. There are two doors, one opens on the cliff, the other opens on the road. The boy staggers into the room as if thrust from behind. Peter follows. He pulls down the boy's fishing clothes which were neatly stacked on a shelf.*

Peter          Lay off the blubbering. We can be
                    Friends when the town's not standing by.
                    Not happy youngster? O the salt
                    Drowns 'em all, we'll keep afloat.
                    You're a landlubber this coast
                    Depresses with its muddy ghosts
                    Of withered trees and with the bleak
                    Ugliness in the ebb tide's wake.
                    You'll discover by and by
                    What this leads to is the sea.
                    Here's your sea boots. Take those bright
                    And fancy buckles off your feet.

*(He throws the sea boots down in front of the boy.)*

                    Here's your oilskin and sou'wester.
                    Stir your pins, we'll get ready!
                    Here's the jersey Ellen knitted,
                    With the anchor that she patterned.

*(He gives the boy the jersey. It has a large red anchor embroidered on the chest.)*

Peter          We shall sail. When we cast off,
                    O we'll gulp the salt of life.
                    While we round the point you'll shout
                    To hide the terror in your heart.
                    When the gunwale dips and waves
                    Leap upon us from above,
                    And the lonely seagulls cry
                    You'll be frightened. So shall I.
                    You'll discover by and by

What this ends in is the sea.

*(The boy's head drops. He is crying again. Peter shakes his shoulder savagely.)*

        I'll tear the collar off your neck.
        Sorry. Don't take fright, boy. Stop.

*(The boy sobs convulsively. Peter tries to soothe him.)*

Peter      *(changes tone)*
        In dreams I've built myself some kindlier home
        Warm in my heart and in a golden calm
        Where there is no more fear and no more storm.
        Where she would soon forget her schoolhouse ways
        Forget the labour of our weary days
        Wrapped round in kindness like September haze.
        The learned at their books have no more store
        Of wisdom than we'd close behind our door.
        Compared with us the rich man would be poor.
        I've seen in stars the life that we might share:
        Fruit in the garden, children by the shore,
        And whitened doorstep, and a woman's care.
        But thinking builds what thinking can disown.
        Dead fingers stretch out to tear it down.
        I hear my father and the one that drowned
        Calling, there is no peace, there is no stone
        In the earth's thickness to make you a home,
        That you can build with and remain alone.

*(He stops. The boy watches him in fascinated horror: and Peter turns on him suddenly.)*

        Sometimes I see two devils in this hut.
        They're here now by the cramp under my heart –
        My father and the boy I had
        As prentice until you arrived.
        They sit there and their faces shine like flesh.
        Their mouths are open, but I close my ears.
        We're by ourselves young prentice. Shall we then
        Make a pact before they come?

*(In the distance can be heard the song of the neighbours coming up*

*the hill.)*

Chorus *(off)*    Now is gossip put on trial,
                Now the rumours either fail
                Or are shouted in the wind
                Sweeping furious through the land.

                Now the liars shiver, for
                Now if they've cheated we shall know
                We shall strike and strike to kill
                At the slander or the sin.

*(Peter goes to the street door, and looks out.)*

Peter          There's an odd procession here.
                Parson and Swallow coming near.

Chorus *(off)*    Now the whisperer stands out
                To be confronted by the fact
                Bring the branding iron and knife
                What's done now is done for life.

*(The boy doesn't move. Peter flings the other door open. Suddenly he turns on the boy.)*

                Wait! You've been talking.
                You and that bitch were gossiping.
                What lies have you been telling?
                The Borough's climbing up the road.
                To get me. Me! O I'm not scared
                I'll send them off with a flea in their ear.
                I'll show them. Grimes ahoy!
                You sit there silently. Your eyes
                Are like Ellen's womanly.
                You sit there yearning like a girl
                Whose face has the wrong tale to tell.
                You sit there. Will you move
                Or shall I make you dance?
                Yes. We'll take the lesser risk
                Down the cliff side to the deck.

*(The boy scrambles through the cliff door to the ledge.)*

                Careful, or you'll break your neck.

Come on. I'll pitch the stuff down.

*(Pitches ropes and nets.)*

Now
Close your eyes and down you go.

*There is a knocking at the other door. Peter turns towards it, then retreats. Meanwhile the boy climbs out. When Peter is between the two doors the boy screams and falls out of sight. Peter runs to the cliff door, feels for his grip and then swings after him. The cliff-side door is open. The street door still resounds with the Rector's knock. Then it opens and the Rector puts his head round the door.*

| | |
|---|---|
| Rector | Peter Grimes! Nobody here? |
| Swallow | What about the other door? |

*(They go and look out. Silence for a moment.)*

| | |
|---|---|
| Rector | Was this a recent landslide? |
| Swallow | Yes. |
| Rector | It makes almost a precipice. |
| | How deep? |
| Swallow | Say fifty feet. |
| Rector | Dangerous to have the door open. |
| Ned | He used to keep his boat down there. |
| | Maybe they've both gone fishing. |
| Rector | Yet |
| | His hut is reasonably kept. |
| | Here's order. Here's skill. |

*(Swallow draws the moral.)*

| | |
|---|---|
| Swallow | The whole affair gives Borough talk its – shall |
| | I say quietus? Here we come pell-mell, |
| | Expecting to find out we know not what |
| | And all we find's a neat and empty hut. |
| | Gentlemen, take this to your wives: |
| | Less interference in our private lives. |
| Rector | There's no point certainly in staying here, |
| | And will the last comer please to close the door. |

*(They go out – all save Balstrode who has come in late who goes to the cliff side door, looks down, then closes it carefully.)*

CURTAIN

## Act III
## Scene 1

*Scene as in Act One, a few days later. The time is summer evening. One of the season's subscription dances is taking place in the Moot Hall which is brightly lit and from which we can hear the rhythm of the dancers' feet. 'The Boar', too, is brightly lit and, as the dance goes on, there will be a regular passage – of the males at any rate – from the Moot Hall to the Inn. The stage is empty when the curtain rises but presently there is a little squeal and one of the nieces scampers down the exterior staircase of the Moot Hall closely followed by Swallow. They haven't got very far before the other niece appears at the top of the Moot Hall stairs. A Barn Dance is being played.*

| | |
|---|---|
| Swallow | *(to Niece 1)* Assign your prettiness to me, |
| | I'll seal the deed and take no fee, |
| | My signature, your graceful mark |
| | Both are witnessed by the abetting dark. |
| | Both Nieces Together we are safe |
| | As any wedded wife. |
| | Safety in number lies |
| | A man is always lighter |
| | His conversation brighter |
| | Provided that the tête-à-tête's in threes. |
| Swallow | Assign your prettiness to me |
| | I'll call it real property: |
| | Your sister shan't insist upon |
| | Her stay of execution. |
| Nieces | Save us from lonely men, |
| | They're like a broody hen |
| | With habits but with no ideas; |
| | But given choice of pleasures |
| | They show their coloured feathers |
| | Provided that the tête-à-tête's in threes. |
| Swallow | I shall seek powers to have her moved; |
| | You have first option on my love. |
| | If my appeal should be ignored |
| | I'll take it to the House of Lords. |
| Nieces | Pairing is all to blame |

|          | For awkwardness and shame,                        |
|----------|---------------------------------------------------|
|          | And all these manly sighs and tears               |
|          | Which wouldn't be expended                        |
|          | If people condescended                            |
|          | Always to have their tête-à-têtes in threes.      |
| Swallow  | Assign your prettiness to me,                     |
|          | We'll make an absolute decree                     |
|          | Of quiet enjoyment which you'll bless             |
|          | By sending sister somewhere else.                 |
| Niece 2  | Ned Keene is chasing me, gives me no peace.       |
| Swallow  | He went to 'The Boar' to have a glass             |
|          | Sister and I will join him there.                 |
|          | If you don't want Ned you'd better stay here.     |

*(He opens the inn door. Niece is about to enter when –)*

| Niece 1 | They're all watching. I must wait |
|---------|-----------------------------------|
|         | Until Auntie's turned her back.   |

*(She runs away to join her sister and leaves Swallow holding the door open.)*

Swallow    Bah!

He goes into 'The Boar' alone. The barn dance stops – applause.

The sisters are half way up the stairs when Ned Keene comes out of the Moot Hall at the top of the stairs. They fly, giggling, and hide behind of the boats on the shore.

Three boats can be seen as at the end of Act One.

Ned    *(calls after them)* Ahoy.

He is half way to their hiding place when a peremptory voice stops him in mid career. Mrs Sedley is at the top of the Moot Hall stairs.

A slow waltz starts from the Moot Hall.

| Mrs Sedley | Mr Keene. Can you spare a moment?        |
|------------|------------------------------------------|
|            | I've something to say that's more than urgent, |
|            | About Peter Grimes and that boy.         |

*(She is downstairs by now and has him buttonholed.)*

|  | Neither of them was seen yesterday.       |
|--|-------------------------------------------|
|  | It's more than suspicion now, it's fact.  |

|            | The boy's disappeared. |
| Ned        | Do you expect me to act |
|            | Like a Bow Street runner or a constable? |
| Mrs Sedley | For two days I've kept my eyes open, |
|            | For two days I've said nothing; |
|            | Only watched and taken notes |
|            | Pieced clue to clue and bit by bit |
|            | Reconstructed all the crime. |
|            | Everything points to Peter Grimes. |
|            | He is the murderer. |
| Ned        | You're far too ready |
|            | To yell blue murder. Where's the body? |
| Mrs Sedley | In the sea the prentice lies |
|            | Whom nobody has seen for days. |
|            | Murder most foul it is |
|            | Eerie I find it |
|            | My skin's a prickly heat |
|            | Blood cold behind it |
|            | In midnight's loneliness |
|            | And thrilling quiet |
|            | The history I trace |
|            | The stifling secret. |
|            | Murder most foul it is... |
|            | And I shall share it. |

| Ned        | *(who is getting bored, thirsty and angry)* |
|            | Are you mad old woman |
|            | Or is it too much laudanum? |
| Mrs Sedley | *(like a cross-examining counsel)* |
|            | Has Peter Grimes been seen? |
| Ned        | He's away. |
| Mrs Sedley | And the boy? |
| Ned        | They're fishing, likely. |
| Mrs Sedley | Has his boat been in? |
| Ned        | Why should it? |
| Mrs Sedley | His hut abandoned. |
| Ned        | I'm dry. Good night. |

*The waltz stops. He breaks away from her grasp, goes into 'The Boar' and bangs the door after him.*

Dr. Crabbe and the Rector and other burgesses come down the Moot Hall stairs. Mrs Sedley retires into the shadow of the boats.

A Hornpipe starts from the Moot Hall.

| | |
|---|---|
| Burgess | Come along, Doctor – *(indicates 'The Boar')* |
| | We're not wanted here, we oldsters. |
| Burgesses | Good night – it's time for bed. |
| | Good night. Good night. Good night, good people, |
| | good night. |
| Rector | I looked in a moment, the company's gay, |
| | With pretty young women and youths on the spree, |
| | All parched like my roses, but now the sun's down |
| | I'll water my roses and leave you the wine. |
| Burgesses | Good night. Good night. Good night, good people, |
| | good night. |
| Rector | Good night, Dr. Crabbe, all good friends good night. |
| | Don't let the ladies keep company too late. |
| | Give my love to the girls, wish luck to the men. |
| | I'll water my roses and leave you the wine. |

*(He goes outs waving.)*

| | |
|---|---|
| Burgesses | Good night. Good night. Good night, good people, |
| | good night. |

*(The Hornpipe fades out.)*

| | |
|---|---|
| Mrs Sedley | *(still in the boat shadow, goes on with her brooding):* |
| | Crime, which my study is |
| | Sweetens my thinking. |
| | Men who can breach the peace |
| | And kill convention – |
| | So many guilty ghosts |
| | With stealthy body |
| | Trouble my midnight thoughts... |
| | Crime is my study. |

*Ellen and Balstrode come up slowly from the beach. It is clear they have been in earnest talk. As they approach Balstrode shines his lantern on the name of the nearest boat: 'Boy Billy'.*

*Mrs Sedley doesn't show herself.*

| Ellen | Is the boat in? |
| Balstrode | More than an hour. |
| | Peter seems to have disappeared |
| | Not in his boat, not in his hut. |
| Ellen | *(holds out the boy's jersey)* |
| | This I found |
| | Down by the tide-mark. |

(It is getting dark. To see the garment properly Balstrode holds it to his lantern.)

| Balstrode | The boy's? |
| Ellen | My broidered anchor on the chest. |
| *(meditative)* | |

Embroidery in childhood was
A luxury of idleness
A coil of silken thread that gave
Dreams of a silk and satin life.
Now my broidery affords
The clue whose meaning we avoid.
My hand remembered its old skill –
These stitches tell a curious tale.
I remember I was brooding
On the fantasies of children
And dreamt that only by wishing I
Could bring some silk into their lives.
Now my broidery affords
The clue whose meaning we avoid.

*(The jersey is wet. Balstrode wrings the water out.)*

| Balstrode | We'll find him, maybe give a hand. |
| Ellen | We have no power to help him now. |
| Balstrode | We have the power. We have the power. |
| | In the black moment |
| | When your friend suffers |
| | Unearthly torment |
| | We cannot turn our backs. |
| | When horror breaks one heart |
| | All hearts are broken. |

| | |
|---|---|
| Ellen | We shall be there with him. |
| Balstrode | Nothing to do but wait |
| | Now the solution |
| | Is beyond life – beyond |
| | Dissolution. |

*(They go out together. When they have gone Mrs Sedley goes quickly to the inn door.)*

| | |
|---|---|
| Mrs Sedley | *(calling through the door)* |
| | Mr Swallow, Mr Swallow. |
| | I want the lawyer Swallow. |
| Auntie | *(off)* What do you want? |
| Mrs Sedley | I want the lawyer Swallow. |
| Auntie | He's busy. |
| Mrs Sedley | Fetch him please, this is official. |
| | Business about the Borough criminal. |
| Auntie | My customers come here for peace, |
| | From you and all such nuisances. |
| Mrs Sedley | This is an insult! |
| Auntie | You will find |
| | So long as I'm here I speak my mind. |
| Mrs Sedley | I'll have you know your place, |
| | You baggage! |
| Auntie | My customers come here for peace, |
| | They take their drink, they take their ease! |
| Swallow | *(coming out)* What is the matter? |
| Mrs Sedley | *(points dramatically)* Look! |
| Swallow | I'm short- |
| | Sighted you know. |
| Mrs Sedley | It's Grimes's boat. |
| Swallow | That's different. Hey. |

*(Shouts into 'The Boar'.)*

| | |
|---|---|
| | Is Hobson there? |
| Hobson | *(off)* Ay, Ay, sir. |
| Swallow | As the mayor, |
| | I ask you to find Peter Grimes. |
| | ake whatever help you need. |
| Hobson | Now what I claims |

|          | Is that he's out at sea. |
| Swallow  | *(points)* His boat. |
| Hobson   | We'll send a posse to his hut. |
| Swallow  | If he's not there you'll search the shore, |
|          | The marsh, the fields, the streets, the Borough. |
| Hobson   | Ay, Ay, sir. |

*(He goes into 'The Boar' hailing.)*

| Mrs Sedley | Crime – that's my study – is |
|            | By cities hoarded. |
|            | The Borough's larcenies |
|            | Are mostly sordid. |
|            | Rarely are country minds |
|            | Lifted to murder |
|            | The noblest of the crimes |
|            | Which are my study. |
|            | And now the crime is here |
|            | And I am ready. |

Hobson comes out with Boles and other fishermen.

*When the news reaches the Moot Hall and pub, the people crowd on to the beach.*

| Chorus | Who holds himself apart |
|        | Lets his pride rise |
|        | Him who despises us |
|        | We despise. |
|        | Now cruelty becomes |
|        | His enterprise. |
|        | Him who despises us |
|        | We despise. |

*(The people [still shouting] scatter in all directions.)*

Peter Grimes! Grimes!

CURTAIN

## Act III
## Scene 2

*Scene as in Scene One. Some hours later. The dance is over and the
Borough is out hunting. Peter alone by his boat in the changeful light
of a cloud-swept moon. There is a distant fog-horn. (The orchestra is
silent.) As before we can hear shouting, now in the far distance:*

| | |
|---|---|
| Voices | Peter Gri-imes – Peter Gri-imes! |
| | Grimes! |
| Peter | Quietly. Here you are. You're home. |
| | This breakwater with splinters torn |
| | By winds, is where your father took |
| | You by the hand to this same boat |
| | Leaving your home for the same sea |
| | Where he died and you're going to die. |
| | Quietly. Here you are. You're home. |
| | You're not to blame that he went down. |
| | It was his weakness that let go. |
| | He was too weak. Were you to know? |
| | He was too weak, and so the sea |
| | Engulfed him, and you're going to die. |
| Voices | Peter Grimes, Peter Grimes! |
| Peter | You shouters there – I've made it right. |
| | It was my conscience, my fate |
| | Got rid of him. If you who call |
| | Don't understand, old Swallow will. |

*(Ellen comes in. His appearance startles here.)*

| | |
|---|---|
| Ellen | Peter! |
| Peter | Was it you who called? |
| | I'm alone now as you foretold. |
| | I am alone. The argument |
| | Is finished and the money spent. |
| | The drinking's over, wild oats sown. |
| | You hear them shouting? I'm alone. |
| Ellen | The cries you hear are in your mind, |
| | Hallucination. |
| Voice | *(very near and loud)* Peter Grimes. |

| Peter | You hear it? |
| Ellen | No |
| Peter | Will you also take |
| | Away my smell and touch and taste? |
| | ou hear them call my name, the sky |
| | Hears it, so do the stars, the sea. |

*(He shouts back at them.)*

| | Peter Grimes. Peter Grimes. Peter Grimes. |
| | Peter Gri-i-i-mes. |
| Voices | Peter Grimes. |
| Peter | Peter Grimes. Peter Grimes. |
| Ellen | *(soothes and calms him)* |
| | Your spasm's over now. The cool |
| | Sea will tranquilise your soul. |
| | Peter. I'm going to fetch Balstrode. |
| | He'll help you to prepare your boat. |

*Peter, left alone, sings in a tone almost like a prolonged sobbing. The voices shouting 'Peter Grimes' can still be heard but more distantly and more sweetly.*

| Peter | Prentice forgive. I did not mean |
| | That your need should give way to mine. |
| | Young prentice come |
| | Young prentice home. |
| | Young prentice if your candle flame |
| | Of little life dies in the dawn |
| | Young prentice come |
| | Young prentice home. |

*(Balstrode comes in followed by Ellen, who stands apart.)*

| Balstrode | Come on. I'll help you with the boat. |
| Ellen | No. |
| Balstrode | Sail out till you lose sight of the Moot Hall, then sink her. You'll know what to do. Goodbye Peter. |

*Together they push the boat down the slope of the shore. Balstrode comes back and waves goodbye. He takes Ellen who is sobbing quietly, calms her and leads her carefully down the main street home.*

*The men pushing the boat out has been the cue for the orchestra to start playing again. Now dawn begins.*

*Dawn comes to the Borough by a gentle sequence of sights and sounds. A candle is lighted and shines through a bare window. A shutter is drawn back.*

*Hobson and his posse meet severally on the green by the Moot Hall. They gossip together, shake their heads, indicate the hopelessness of the search, extinguish their lanterns, and while some turn home, others go to the boats. Nets are brought down from the houses by fisherwives. Cleaners open the front door of the Inn and begin to scrub the step.*

*Dr. Crabbe comes from a confinement case with his black bag. He yawns and stretches. Nods to the cleaners. The Rector comes to early morning prayer. Mrs Sedley follows. Ned Keene draws the shutters of his shop. Mr Swallow comes out and speaks to the fishermen.*

| | |
|---|---|
| Swallow | There's a boat sinking out at sea, |
| | Coastguard reports. |
| Fisherman | Within reach? |
| Swallow | No. |

*(Fishermen go with Swallow to the beach and look out. One of them has a glass.)*

| | |
|---|---|
| Auntie | What is it? |
| Boles | Nothing I can spy. |
| Auntie | One of these rumours. |

*(Nieces emerge and begin to polish the brasses outside 'The Boar.')*

| | |
|---|---|
| Chorus | To those who pass the Boro' sounds betray. |
| | The cold beginning of another day |
| | And houses sleeping by the waterside |
| | Wake to the measured ripple of the tide; |
| | Or measured cadence of the lads who tow |
| | Some entered hoy to fix her in her row, |
| | Or hollow sound that from the passing bell |
| | To some departed spirit bids farewell. |
| | In ceaseless motion comes and goes the tide |
| | Flowing it fills the channel vast and wide |

Then back to sea with strong majestic sweep
It rolls in ebb yet terrible and deep.

*(By now the morning life of the Borough is in full flood.)*

*During the Chorus the* CURTAIN *slowly falls.*

# Deleted 'Mad Song' from *Peter Grimes* (1945)

Home? Would you give a comet room
Beneath your eaves and call it home?
This God who made the world and said
Let there be light and darkness made
And breathed a self-degrading love
Into the dust and called it life
This is your God of love – but I
Climb to his heaven to defy.

Here is an eye that sees the plan
For the enfeeblement of man
And a will strong enough to roll
Creation back for a new man's soul.
O I can breathe the naked dawn
And drink the sea to pull God down
Deny his laws, like fire consume
The shame that breathes in all things human.

O would you give a comet room
Between your breasts and call it home?

# Notes

## Part I Poems

'An Elegy' (1931). First published in Arnold Rattenbury ed., 'Poems of Montagu Slater', *Renaissance and Modern Studies* XX (1976), pp. 123–25. Slater Papers, Tw T 1/1/19. The final line here is based on Slater's final typescript, and differs slightly from that given by Rattenbury ('give up the kingdom of all visible things').

'Love, We Can Lie Back' Undated. First published in Rattenbury ed., 'Poems of Montagu Slater', p. 123. The original is missing from the Slater Papers.

'Cock Crow.' Undated. First published in Rattenbury ed., 'Poems', p. 125. Slater Papers, Tw T 1/1/35.

'The Ebb and Flow of the Moon.' Undated. First published in Rattenbury ed., 'Poems', p. 126. Slater Papers, Tw T 1/1/42.

'The Fear.' Undated. First published in Rattenbury ed., 'Poems', p. 126; also published in Edgell Rickword and John St. John eds., 'Montagu Slater: A Group of Occasional Poems', *New Reasoner 4* (Spring 1958), p. 84. The text here reflects Slater's final typescript version, Slater Papers, Tw T 1/1/44.

'Incitement to Disaffection: a Fragment.' Undated. First published, in a slightly different version, in Rattenbury ed., 'Poems', pp. 128–29. This version reflects the manuscript in Tw T /1/52. The poem shares its title with an editorial in the first issue of *Left Review* written in protest against the Incitement to Disaffection Bill, widely termed 'the Sedition Bill', which made it into a criminal offence to attempt to 'seduce' a member of the armed forces from 'duty or allegiance' to the crown. The Bill received Royal Assent on 16 November 1934. Unsigned, *Left Review* (October 1934), p. 37. Humphy Davy (1778–1829), British chemist and inventor of the miners' Safety Lamp.

'In the Beginning: *A Broken Narrative.*' Undated. Originally signed 'Charles Slater' and published in the first issue of *Left Review* (October 1934), pp. 30–33. 'Churchill gazette'; reference to the *British Gazette*, the newspaper produced by the government during the 1926 General Strike, edited by Chancellor of the Exchequer, Winston Churchill.

'The Hunter and the Hunted.' Undated. First published in Rattenbury ed., 'Poems', pp. 133–34. This version reflects Slater's final typescript, Slater Papers, Tw T 1/1/48/1.

'Where My Bones Rest.' Undated. Published in the *New Statesman* (14/4/51). Slater Papers, Tw T 1/1/22.

'The Ambassador.' Undated. Slater Papers, Tw T 1/1/28.

'A Ballad from Korea (based on two newspaper correspondents' dispatches).' 29/4/51, Slater Papers, Tw T 1/1/29.

'Character Equals Situation.' Undated, first published in Rickword ed., 'Montagu Slater: A Group of Poems', *New Reasoner 4* (Spring 1958), p. 83. The text here reflects Slater's final typescript version, Slater Papers, Tw T 1/1/32/10.

'Exercise with a Broad Nib.' Undated, originally published in an unidentified periodical adjacent to George Macbeth's 'On Reading "The Concept of Mind."' Clipping in Slater Papers, Tw T 1/1/43.

'Helen Was Not Up Was She.' Undated, Slater Papers, Tw T 1/1/47. Helen of Troy, considered the most beautiful woman in the world and wife of Spartan king, Menelaus. In myth, Helen's abduction by the Trojan Paris precipitated the Trojan war. Priam, Paris's father, was King of Troy.

'Now Praise....' Undated. Slater Papers, Tw T 1/1/68.

'The Obituary' and 'The Answer'. Undated. Slater clearly considered these poems as a pair. Slater Papers, Tw T 1/1/70.

'The Pitfall.' Undated. Slater Papers, Tw T 1/1/78.

'St Venus's Eve.' Undated. Slater Papers, Tw T 1/1/86.

'A Sentence of Judges.' Undated. Slater Papers, Tw T 1/1/87; there is a typographical error in Slater's final typescript version ('general in cocks (sic) feathers proud'; I have added an apostrophe: 'cocks' feathers').

'The Spirit Kills.' Undated. Slater Papers, Tw T 1/1/91.

'To Chloe with an Old Valentine.' Undated. Slater Papers, Tw T 1/1/96.

'When I Awake.' Undated. Slater Papers Tw T 1/1/100.

'Untitled.' Undated. First published as 'The Other Encounter' in Rickword ed., 'Group of Poems', p. 81. This version reflects Slater's final typescript version. Slater Papers, Tw T 1/1/105.

'Poems from an Ibo Sequence': 'Iboland', 'A Dark Place under the Trees', 'This is our Love Child', 'Men and Women Almost Equal.' Undated. First published in Clifford Dyment, Montagu Slater, Roy Fuller ed., *New Poems 1952: A PEN Anthology* (London: Michael Joseph, 1952), pp. 90–93. The Slater Papers contain versions of a further five poems: 'Through Sloping Galleries', 'To a Quadroon seen in a Restaurant', 'Chained Convicts at Enugu Crickey Ground' and 'Four Days make an Ibo Week.' Slater Papers, Tw T 1/1/49/1–36.

'On a 17th Century Painting.' Undated. Slater Papers, Tw T 1/1/72. The sacrifice of Isaac by Abraham was widely painted by the Old Masters in the early Seventeenth Century (Rubens, Rembrandt, Caravaggio). I haven't been able to establish which, if any, version Slater has in mind.

'Royal Academy: Special Exhibition.' Undated. First published as 'National Gallery (Special Exhibition)' in Rickword ed., 'Group of Poems', p. 82. The text reflects Slater's final typescript version, Slater Papers, Tw T 1/1/83. Francesco Guardi (1712–1793); member of the Venetian School. The poem is a response to 'Gala Concert' (1782), Bavarian State Paintings Collection.

'Your Touch Has Still.' Undated. First published as 'National Gallery (Permanent Collection)' in Rickword ed., 'Group of Poems', p. 82. This text reflects Slater's final typescript version. Slater Papers, Tw T 1/1/106.

'Past Years.' Undated. Slater Papers, Tw T 1/1/77.


### Part II Songs and Choruses from Dramatic Works

'Ballad.' First published in Rattenbury ed., 'Poems', pp. 127–28. From the play 'Domesday' (dated by Rattenbury as 1933). Playscript in Slater Papers, Tw T 1/2/9. As Rattenbury notes, the play owes much to Jack London's novel *The Iron Heel* (1908).

'Speech for a Fascist', from the play 'Cock Robin', where it is spoken by 'Leader', a figure from the hero's dream. The fourth verse, with the last verse added, recurs as a reprise. First published in Rattenbury ed., 'Poems', pp. 129–30; Playscript in Slater Papers, Tw T 1/2/28.

'Chorus from Easter 1916.' First published in Slater, *Easter 1916* (London: Lawrence & Wishart, 1936), pp. 73–74. The stage directions specify that the chorus should be spoken, 'with a tune in the background, matching its rhythm.' Republished in *Peter Grimes and Other Poems* (London: Bodley Head, 1946), pp. 79–81.

'Mother Comfort'. One of two 'ballads for two voices and piano' set by Benjamin Britten and first performed at the Wigmore Hall on 15 December 1936 by Sophie Wyss and Betty Bannerman. The other ballad was Auden's 'Underneath an Abject Willow'. Published by Boosey & Hawkes in 1937; republished Rattenbury ed., 'Poems', p. 131 and in Boris Ford ed., *Benjamin Britten's poets: the poetry he set to music* (Manchester: Carcanet, 1994), p. 47.

'Chorus from *Stay Down Miner*'. First published in Slater, *New Way Wins: The First Published Version of the Play Originally Entitled Stay Down Miner* (London: Lawrence & Wishart, 1937), pp. 55–56.

'Deleted Song from the mountain scene of *Stay Down Miner*', set by Benjamin Britten for male voices. Published in Slater, New Way Wins, p. viii. A telpher is a coal carrier, suspended on cables.

'Chorus'. Undated. Original source unclear. Possibly from one of the lost 1930s pageants. First published in Rattenbury ed., 'Poems', p. 130. Tw T 1/1/33.

'Women's Chorus'. From 'Towards Tomorrow', a pageant of co-operation, performed Wembley Stadium, July 2, 1938. The pageant script has not yet come to light, but the chorus is in the Slater papers, Tw T 1/1/103. Reprinted in Rattenbury ed., 'Poems, pp. 132–33. In stanza eight, this version reflects Slater's final typescript, rather than the text given by Rattenbury, in which the singular woman is made plural. Rattenbury's text adds a comma after peoples in the penultimate stanza. That change is retained here.

'Chorus.' Reprinted in Rattenbury ed., 'Poems', p. 134. Rattenbury's note says: '1940 or 1941. Subsequently used in "An Agreement of the People", Empress Stadium, June 1942 (in which Philosopher was played by CEM. Joad who wrote his own words')'. The manuscript of the pageant hasn't yet to come to light and there is no version of this chorus in the Slater Papers. There's what seems to be a typographical error in line ten of the Rattenbury text – 'To land on arifileds (sic) made of ice'; that is corrected here, to 'airfields.'

'A Verse for Arthur Benjamin.' Dated 10/11/46/ Whether this poem was ever sent to Arthur Benjamin is not clear. Benjamin (1893–1960) was a composer and Professor of Piano at the Royal College of Music, where he taught the young Britten. Slater Papers, Tw T 1/1/20.

## Part III Libretti and Poetic Dramas

'The Seven Ages of Man.' Performed by Binyon Puppets, with music by Benjamin Britten, at the Mercury Theatre, Notting Hill, London, July 1938. Published in Slater, *Peter Grimes and other Poems* (London: Bodley Head, 1946), pp. 59–71.

'Old Spain.' Performed by Binyon Puppets, with music by Benjamin Britten, at the Mercury Theatre, Notting Hill, London, July 1938. Published in Slater, *Peter Grimes and other Poems* (London: Bodley Head, 1946), pp. 71–79. Hernán Cortés (1485–1547): Spanish conquistador who led the expedition that precipitated the fall of the Aztec Empire. Part of the generation of explorers and conquistadors central to the first stage of the Spanish colonization of the Americas.

'Peter Grimes', first performed at Sadler's Wells, June 1945. Published in Slater, *Peter Grimes and other Poems* (London: Bodley Head, 1946), pp. 11–59.

'Mad Song (deleted from Peter Grimes)'. First published in Edgell Rickword ed., 'Montagu Slater: A Group of Poems', *New Reasoner 4* (Spring 1958), p. 84. Slater Papers, Tw T 1/1/58.